Helion & Company Limited
Unit 8 Amherst Business Centre
Budbrooke Road
Warwick
CV34 5WE
England
Tel. 01926 499 619
Email: info@helion.co.uk
Website: www.helion.co.uk
Twitter: @helionbooks
Visit our blog http://blog.helion.co.uk/

Designed and typeset by Farr out Publications, Wokingham, Berkshire
Cover design Paul Hewitt, Battlefield Design (www.battlefield-design.co.uk)

Cover photo: A warship of the class known in the USSR as Project 1135 Burevestnik, and to NATO as the Krivak I – the class to which Storozhevoy belonged. The Soviet Navy had the practice of regularly changing hull numbers of its ships, it is therefore unclear if this photograph shows Storozhevoy around the time of the mutiny, or sister-ship *Bditelnyy* as of 1971. (US DoD)

Cover artwork: A Tu-16-10-26 bomber with K-10S anti-ship missile. (Artwork by Tom Cooper)

ISBN 978-1-915070-70-8

British Library Cataloguing-in-Publication Data
A catalogue record for this book is available from the British Library

CONTENTS

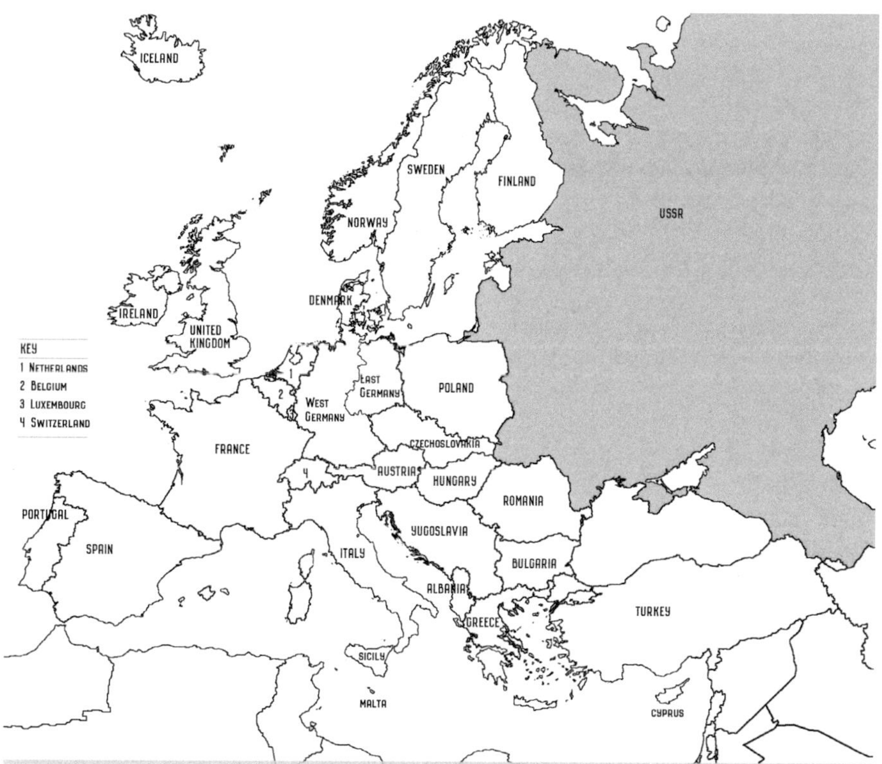

MAP OF EUROPE 1945–1992

Note: In order to simplify the use of this book, all names, locations and geographic designations are as provided in *The Times World Atlas*, or other traditionally accepted major sources of reference, as of the time of described events.

INTRODUCTION

The mutiny on the Soviet Navy warship *Storozhevoy* in 1975 led to perhaps the most dangerous crisis in the Baltic Sea region during the entire Cold War.

Mutinies were not unheard-of phenomena on Soviet naval vessels. But the mutiny on the *Storozhevoy* was unique in that it was not just an expression of dissatisfaction. The ringleader of the mutineers, Valeriy Sablin, was no mere disgruntled sailor but an avowed communist and the ship's political officer. The mutineers dreamt of carrying out a socialist revolution. However, the regime they wanted to overthrow, the Communist Party of the Soviet Union, had itself gained power through revolutionary means – the October Revolution of 1917. As a result, both the Soviet Navy and the Communist Party leadership immediately assumed that the mutineers simply wished to defect to Sweden and the presumed easy life in the West.

At the time of the mutiny, the *Storozhevoy* was temporarily moored in Riga, the capital of the Soviet Republic of Latvia. Sablin's avowed intention was to take the warship to Leningrad, where he expected to receive the support of the Navy and the masses, which in turn would foment a new communist revolution. This was also the story that Sablin after the event presented during his court martial. However, the Soviet leadership regarded the risk that Sablin intended to defect to Sweden, bringing with him a warship of modern design with all its armaments, electronics, communication devices, cipher systems, and code books, as too high to accept. As a result, Soviet supreme leader Leonid Brezhnev ordered the destruction of the *Storozhevoy*. After several dramatic, but ultimately failed, attacks on the *Storozhevoy*, Colonel General Sergey Gulyayev, commander of Naval Aviation of the Baltic Fleet, ordered a missile launch against the *Storozhevoy*, employing the special protocol for the launch of nuclear missiles. The purpose of the launch was to annihilate the warship and its crew, so as to avoid any risk of information loss to the West. However, by then members of the warship's crew had already understood what was underway. They detained Sablin and announced their intention to surrender. The air crews did not know this, and for the duration of two minutes, the fate of everybody in the area hung in the balance. Fortunately, Colonel Arkhip Savinkov, the commanding officer of the bomber unit, never launched the missile, instead claiming a radar malfunction. The mutiny was over.

Due to the very serious implications of the suppressed mutiny, and the difficulties in finding and attacking the *Storozhevoy*, which showed that the combat readiness of the Soviet armed forces was less than desired, the Soviet leadership ordered the participating air crews to destroy any documentation of the incident and stay silent about what had happened. As a result, not even the KGB could later piece together all events of the incident, nor is there information in Soviet archives on all the actions taken. For much of the mutiny, the Soviet pursuit force did not even know the correct location of the *Storozhevoy*. However, the Swedish national signals intelligence (SIGINT) service, the FRA, monitored the entire incident in real time. The Swedish SIGINT reporting enables a detailed, blow-by-blow description of the events surrounding the mutiny. Being real-time intercepts, the reporting is a far more trustworthy source than the later, often embellished accounts previously published. The SIGINT reporting offers a detailed and authoritative account of the mutiny, with supporting evidence from other surviving sources. The use of a full set of sources also enables a detailed understanding of how Western intelligence interpreted and handled the case of the mutiny on the *Storozhevoy*.

The story of the hunt for the *Storozhevoy* formed the immediate inspiration for Thomas L. Clancy, Jr. when he wrote the bestseller novel *The Hunt for Red October*, which soon was made into a Hollywood blockbuster. However, the story also illustrates how even the totalitarian Soviet Union was not immune to dissent and uprisings, and sometimes from surprising quarters. But, even more so, the story of the hunt for the *Storozhevoy* shows why servicemen should remember that it is not always wise to obey orders, especially if the consequences of obeying are impossible to predict, and that despite serving a totalitarian state, many Soviet officers and soldiers could be trusted to do the right thing when calamity threatened.

1
THE SOVIET ARMED FORCES

In 1975, the Soviet Union was one of the world's two superpowers. By this time, Soviet power derived from military might alone. The Soviet Union was not an economic power, nor was it prominent as a manufacturer or in international trade. The country had respectable scientists and produced – and exported – reliable weapons systems but was unable to manufacture competitive consumer goods. In previous decades, Marxists and left-wing radicals around the world had looked up to the Soviet system as an ideological paragon of what a state and society for the working class should look like, but this time had already passed. Following the armed suppression of first unrest in East Germany in 1953, then the Hungarian Uprising in 1956, and finally the Prague Spring in 1968, Soviet-style socialism no longer looked as enticing as in the past.

Most of the Soviet Union's military might was controlled by the Ministry of Defence through the General Staff, which directed the six major arms of service of the Soviet Armed Forces: the Strategic Rocket Forces (Russian: *Raketnyye voyska strategicheskogo naznacheniya*), Ground Forces (*Sukhoputnyye voyska*), National Air Defence Forces (*Voyska protivovozdushoy oborony strany*, *PVO strany* in short), Air Forces (*Voyenno-vozdushnyye sily*), Navy (*Voyenno-morskoy flot*), and as a separate arm of service the Airborne Forces (*Vozdushno-desantnyye voyska*). The arms of service exercised administrative control over the field forces, which in peacetime were deployed in 16 Military Districts (*voyennyy okrug*, pl. *voyennyye okruga*) and four Groups of Forces (primarily the Group of Soviet Forces in Germany, but also the Northern Group of Forces in Poland, the Central Group of Forces in Czechoslovakia, and the Southern Group of Forces in

Hungary), four Fleets (the Northern, Baltic, Black Sea, and Pacific), one Flotilla (the Caspian), two Air Defence Districts (*okruga PVO*, Moscow and Baku), and several independent Air Defence Armies. In addition, the General Staff controlled a host of support services and special troops. In total, the Armed Forces encompassed more than 3,500,000 men and women under arms. All the arms of services had separate chains of command, even when they were deployed in the same geographical area. Moreover, air units were not only divided into the National Air Defence Forces and Air Forces. The Navy included dedicated Naval Aviation (*Aviatsiya voyenno-morskogo flota*) units, distributed among the Fleets.

Moreover, Soviet armed units could be found elsewhere as well. The Committee for State Security (KGB) controlled the intelligence and security services, but also ran the Border Troops (*Pogranichnyye voyska*), which consisted of some 200,000 men under arms in regular ground, naval, and air units which were used to protect the borders. The Ministry of the Interior (MVD) ran the police but also managed paramilitary units known as Internal Troops (*Vnutrenniye voyska*), which encompassed another roughly 260,000 men under arms. Both the Border Troops and the Internal Troops legally formed part of the Armed Forces of the Soviet Union, even though they operated through separate chains of command.

The Soviet Navy

Imperial Russia had maintained a navy since the mid-seventeenth century and often used it to good effect. However, after the Russian Revolution in 1917, the new Soviet power focused its attention on the Red Army (its name until 1946), not the Navy. The Soviet fleets were merely tasked with territorial defence, the protection of those regions of the Soviet Union that were vulnerable to assault from the sea. This was quite understandable, since several Western powers, including Britain and the United States, had landed intervention forces in the Soviet state during the civil war which followed the revolution. The German invasion during the Second World War, too, had showed the Soviet leadership the importance of fielding a strong army. For the early Soviet leaders, including Joseph Stalin (1878–1953), the best use of a navy was in support of the army, which in their view provided the real fighting force.

However, with the onset of the Cold War requirements changed. A nuclear superpower, the Soviet Union could no longer ignore the oceans that surrounded its great landmass. Henceforth, the Navy's missions would still include territorial defence (against enemy bombardment as well as amphibious assault, lessons learned from the Second World War). The Navy would also continue to provide support to the Ground Forces. However, to these missions was added a new one: the mission to provide area defence against incursions into Soviet sea-space by enemy surface vessels and submarines – including, most importantly, those carrying long-range bombers armed with nuclear free-fall bombs and eventually missiles armed with nuclear warheads. With increasing ranges of engagement, it was no longer sufficient to adopt a defensive posture close to the shore. The Navy realised that enemy incursions of the new type would have to be met at some distance from the Motherland, on the high seas. This became particularly urgent after the death of Stalin, following the assumption of full power by Nikita Khrushchev (1894–1971), who ameliorated many of the destructive policies of his predecessor. It is perhaps telling that no transformation of the Navy had been possible under the leadership of Stalin, who when it came to naval matters simply favoured more and larger conventional cruisers, destroyers, and medium-range submarines of the kind which had served him well during the war against Germany. Moreover,

Nikita Sergeyevich Khrushchev, in 1961. (US Department of State)

Stalin also had a history of eliminating those who questioned his policy decisions. Unlike Stalin, Khrushchev saw the need to rely on missiles for national defence. He also wanted to improve the lives of ordinary citizens through a series of economic and agricultural reforms. For these two reasons, Khrushchev ordered major cuts in conventional forces.

Khrushchev also knew that it was necessary to transform the Navy in accordance with the increased responsibilities. In January 1956, he accordingly appointed Sergey Georgiyevich Gorshkov (1910–1988), a veteran of the Second World War, Admiral of the Fleet of the Soviet Union and Commander-in-Chief of the Soviet Navy. Gorshkov served as Commander-in-Chief of the Soviet Navy until 1985. During his time in office, Gorshkov oversaw a massive naval build-up of surface and submarine vessels of new types and armaments and the expansion of the Soviet Navy into a modern force with a global presence. Gorshkov was the chief architect of the naval transformation and modernisation that henceforth took place in the Soviet Union.

Gorshkov's Naval Reforms

Gorshkov and his team early on realised that in the 1950s, the primary naval threat to the Soviet Union derived from American carrier task forces which could move long-distance bombers armed with nuclear weapons into range of the Soviet landmass. The conventional naval setup which derived from the Second World War was insufficient to counter the new threat. Gorshkov and his team accordingly introduced the first change in direction of the Soviet Navy since the Revolution: the introduction of what is best termed the anti-carrier programme. Realising that it would be difficult to shoot down every hostile long-range bomber, Gorshkov and his team instead chose to concentrate on weapon systems that would be able to destroy the aircraft carrier itself, before it arrived in range of the Soviet Motherland and the carrier's bombers could be ordered into the air. To destroy a carrier was, of course, no easy task, since carriers were huge warships and well-protected by the other ships of the carrier task force.

Sergey Georgiyevich Gorshkov, Admiral of the Fleet of the Soviet Union and Commander-in-Chief of the Soviet Navy. (Open source)

Gorshkov accordingly abandoned the construction of conventional cruisers, destroyers, and medium-range submarines in favour of the introduction of warships armed with missiles. While the new mission was added to the Navy's existing missions, all of which remained, the requirements of modern war meant that the Soviet design bureaus had to introduce new types of armament that would enable the anti-carrier role. For this reason, anti-ship missiles armed with nuclear warheads became a key component of the anti-carrier programme.

Moreover, Gorshkov rebuilt Naval Aviation around a new large force of land-based long-range bombers armed with anti-ship missiles. Henceforth, enemy carrier task forces would be met by a hard-hitting combination of, from the air, long-range Naval Aviation units armed with anti-ship missiles, from the surface, surface warships likewise armed with missiles, and from below, submarines armed with missiles as well as torpedoes.

Colonel General Sergey Arsent'yevich Gulyayev (1918–2000), commander of Naval Aviation of the Baltic Fleet and Hero of the Soviet Union for his exploits during the Second World War, knew exactly how to accomplish his objective. In 1965, he explained the shift in strategy in an article in the influential Soviet naval journal, the *Morskoy sbornik* ('Naval Collection'):

> Naval aviation armed with missiles with nuclear warheads can use its powerful weapons outside the operational range of shipboard surface-to-air missiles and almost beyond the potential range of fighters directed against these aircraft. This permits missile-carrying aviation to carry out effectively the mission of destroying enemy warships and transports at sea, regardless of their anti-aircraft defence systems. Modern naval aviation has great opportunities for executing successful combat operations not only against large surface warships but also against submarines including nuclear-powered ones.[1]

Among the Naval Aviation aircraft developed to deal with the carrier threat the primary position was held by the Tupolev Tu-16K bomber (ASCC/NATO-codename 'Badger C'), each armed with a powerful Kometa K-10 guided anti-ship missile. We will see that this particular weapon system played a prominent role during the 1975 Soviet Navy mutiny.

Official photograph of Admiral of the Fleet of the Soviet Union Gorshkov. He oversaw the expansion of the Soviet Navy into a global force during the Cold War. (Soviet Ministry of Defence)

Then, in the early 1960s, a new major threat arose. The mission remained the countering of seaborne nuclear delivery systems, yet the focus began to change. In 1960, the first submarine-launched ballistic missile (SLBM)-armed submarines entered service with the U.S. Navy. This was the Ethan Allen-class submarine, with an armament of 16 Polaris missiles. The first unit was declared operational in November 1960. Henceforth, the Soviets realised, it was no longer sufficient to interdict and destroy the American aircraft carriers; it would also be necessary to locate and destroy the American missile-armed submarines which operated beyond Soviet sea-space, notably in the Norwegian Sea, the northern reaches of the North Sea, and the eastern Mediterranean.

Gorshkov and his team responded by initiating another major defence programme, that of anti-submarine warfare (ASW).

In the words of Robert B. Bathurst, a Western naval analyst:

> The history of Soviet ASW efforts does not begin until the late 1950s because until then there was no real ASW problem. There was no requirement to protect convoys in coastal zones and there was not any great prospect of a submarine threat. Because there was no need to protect shipping on the high seas there was no concept of sea control except for the defensive rings in the Baltic, Black and Okhotsk seas. The Polaris threat abruptly forced the Soviet Navy to expand its operational art. New classes of ships, submarines, and airplanes were developed and became operational in the second half of the 1960s as the Soviets, to meet the threat, adopted an operational doctrine of combined systematic employment of all existing forces for antisubmarine warfare.[2]

Soviet naval theorists based the anti-submarine warfare programme on previous experiences, in particular those of the Second World War. This led to them to conclude that anti-submarine warfare depended on the combined employment of all means for anti-submarine warfare, including a combination of surface vessels and aircraft.[3]

Moreover, the Soviet Navy also began regular deployments of naval units to the aforementioned regions where Polaris-class submarines operated, which hitherto had not formed part of the traditional Soviet defensive zone. The anti-submarine warfare programme consisted of both naval and air assets. It also gave rise to a new major construction effort of new classes of surface ships. In fact, the class of ships to which the *Storozhevoy* belonged (together with several other classes of surface vessels) can be said to be typical of Gorshkov's new focus on the anti-submarine warfare programme. Indeed, the Soviet Navy was less traditional and more willing to adapt to the new circumstances than most Western navies. For instance, with the introduction of guided missile armament, Gorshkov's team also abandoned the traditional system of ship classification in favour of a more descriptive system based on armament and mission type. Henceforth, a surface warship was referred to as a 'missile cruiser' (Russian: *raketnyy kreyser*, RKR), 'large missile ship' (*bol'shoy raketnyy korabl'*, BRK), or 'small missile ship' (*malyy raketnyy korabl'*, MRK), if she operated as a platform for surface-to-surface anti-ship missiles. If her role was anti-submarine warfare, she was instead called an 'anti-submarine warfare cruiser' (*protivolodochnyy kreyser*, PKR), 'large anti-submarine warfare ship' (*bol'shoy protivolodochnyy korabl'*, BPK), or 'small anti-submarine warfare ship' (*malyy protivolodochnyy korabl'*, MPK). Unlike the more tradition-bound Western navies, the Soviets no longer talked about destroyers and frigates. For this reason, Western naval analysts for years dithered over whether a ship such as the *Storozhevoy* should be designated a destroyer, missile destroyer, or frigate. Incidentally, it should be noted that Soviet ship classes were principally designed for offensive operations against either surface ships or submarines. Thus, they were primarily, or exclusively, armed with surface-to-surface missiles (SSM), not surface-to-air missiles (SAM). Neither of these classes were primarily intended for air defence operations, which was more efficiently handled by land-based air units.

Gorshkov explained:

> In the quest for ways of developing our navy, we avoided simply copying the fleet of the most powerful sea power of the world. The composition of the navy, its weapons, ship designs, and organization of forces were determined primarily by the missions which the political leadership of the country assigned to the armed forces and consequently also to the navy, by the country's economic resources, and also by the conditions under which the navy had to accomplish these missions.[4]

Despite Gorshkov's explanation, Western naval analysts often failed to understand his reforms, instead assuming that the Soviets merely copied the navies of the West, and in particular the U.S. Navy. One of the few Western naval analysts who did perceive what happened in the Soviet Union, the aforementioned Robert B. Bathurst, noted that:

> The United States has been concerned in a traditional way with its ability to maintain sea lines of communication to Europe for the resupply of NATO. The Soviets . . . understood this as simply part of the overall strategy of preparing for the decisive war to destroy the socialist camp. Consequently, Soviet tactics involved moving out the perimeter of their defense in accordance with a strategic theory of defense zones. . . . In the West it was not assumed that the Soviets really believed what they were saying about our intention to unleash a war for the destruction of the socialist camp. Other explanations were required, and most often they centered on the assumption that the Soviets themselves were preparing for an aggressive war, primarily one to break our sea lines of communication. The fact that they did not construct ships that seemed suitable for that mission was a constant mystery ... As the Soviets could not be credited with believing the reality of their own positions – it was assumed that they were operating with perceptions that fit our assumptions and not theirs – it was widely believed that they could not be serious about what they said. That assumption underlay much of our strategic and political thinking.[5]

What Bathurst argued against was the tendency to assume that Soviet plans and strategies were based on the same assumptions as those in the West (an analytical cognitive trap known as mirror-imaging). He also, correctly, argued than any analysis based on mirror-imaging was faulty. Soviet naval developments were never quite as slow as was commonly believed in the West. To cite Bathurst again:

> The Soviets were the first to begin building submarines modularly (that is in sections that were then welded together); in the early fifties the Soviets perfected the air-to-surface missile carried by the *Badger* bomber and introduced by 1956 a reconnaissance and strike aircraft with a range of 3,500 miles without refueling; in 1956 the Soviet *Zulu*-class submarine put to sea with a 250-mile ballistic missile to be followed by the first of a series of nuclear-propelled ballistic missile submarines, the *Hotel* class; in November 1957 the first *Sputnik* flew, and it was obviously designed for military, including naval reconnaissance uses. It was not until 1959 that *George Washington*, the United States first nuclear submarine FBM, was launched with sixteen 1,100-mile Polaris A1 missiles. The world's first surface-to-surface missile on a surface ship appeared on the *Kildin* which became operational

> in 1959. The first submarine with surface-to-surface missiles was the *Whiskey* class that appeared in 1958 and went through some modifications before the more sophisticated version, the *Juliet*, appeared in 1962.
>
> Furthermore, it should be recalled that the Soviets had begun writing about the revolution in military science at least as early as 1960. They were quite obviously oriented to the technical and operational changes that the possibility of missiles had introduced into naval warfare long before some Western navies, including our own, fully accommodated them.[6]

One could easily argue that modern-day Western analysis of current Russian strategies and plans frequently suffers from the same problem as its Cold War-equivalent.

To the Soviets, coastal defence involved a layered defensive strategy. Missile cruisers and large missile ships would, together with the large submarine fleet, defend against enemy surface intrusions in open waters and with a particular emphasis on carrier task forces. In a similar manner, anti-submarine warfare cruisers and large anti-submarine warfare ships would defend against sub-surface intrusions in the same waters. Closer to the shore, small missile ships would engage surface intruders, while small anti-submarine warfare ships handled the sub-surface environment. Meanwhile, fast, mobile units of yet smaller vessels, each known as a 'missile boat' (*raketnyy kater*, RKA) or 'torpedo boat' (*torpednyy kater*, TKA), would operate in support, often in conjunction with vessels of similar or slightly larger size, each designated as a patrol ship (*storozhevoy korabl'*, SKR). Most of the vessels intended for operations close to the shore were capable of minelaying in addition to their primary mission. Meanwhile, land-based air units would handle general reconnaissance as well as anti-submarine warfare duties, provide air defence, and with regard to intruding carrier forces, carry out air strikes with missiles armed with nuclear warheads. Any intruder would meet a multifaceted, hostile environment.

By the mid-1970s, Gorshkov's initiatives were mostly completed. The anti-carrier programme and the subsequent anti-submarine warfare programme had expanded the Soviet Navy into a powerful, modern ocean-going force. In 1975, the Soviet Union possessed a powerful fleet of submarines, including those armed with ballistic missiles, a couple of helicopter cruisers, and a soon-to-be operational aircraft carrier. At this time, Gorshkov wrote, clearly with some pride, about the utility to the Soviet state of his blue-water navy:

> We may assert that a state bounded by the sea, which does not have a navy corresponding to its importance in the world, thereby shows its relative economic weakness. Thus, each ship of a navy is a relative indication of the level of development of science, technology, and industry in a given country and an indicator of its real military might.[7]

Nonetheless, the Navy's emphasis remained on coastal defence of the Motherland. For this purpose, a major share of the force consisted of missile cruisers and missile ships on the one hand and anti-submarine warfare cruisers and anti-submarine warfare ships on the other. These were supplemented and supported by the aforementioned fast missile boats and torpedo boats.

Yet, there were subtle differences between the four Fleets. The Northern Fleet, based in Severomorsk in the Arctic Kola Peninsula, focused on ocean-going anti-submarine warfare units and was also the home of most nuclear-powered submarines. The Black Sea Fleet, with headquarters in Sevastopol, had begun operations in the Mediterranean. In comparison, the Pacific Fleet, based in Vladivostok, which had developed into a blue-water fleet under Stalin remained geographically hemmed in by the Japanese islands and the Korean Peninsula. For this reason, it by this time received few modern ocean-going warships. As for the oldest of the Soviet Fleets, the Baltic, with its headquarters in Kaliningrad and primary port in Baltiysk, it had seemingly changed little. Still focused on coastal defence against the Soviet Union's host of enemies on the Western front, it did not openly display the same interest in ocean-going anti-submarine warfare operations as did the Northern Fleet. Nor did its units regularly deploy to foreign waters, as the Black Sea Fleet did in the Mediterranean. NATO observers frequently dismissed the Baltic Fleet as a 'mere coastal defence force'.[8] Indeed, we will see that US intelligence focused elsewhere, which would suggest that the Baltic held little of interest. Yet, it will also be shown that units of the Baltic Fleet were quite able to operate on the open sea and occasionally strayed far beyond the Baltic. Besides, the comparative inattention displayed by US intelligence in the Baltic was not a sign of neglect, but of the existing close co-operation between US intelligence on the one hand and the intelligence services of partner countries such as West Germany, Denmark, and last but not least, Sweden, with which the United States since 1952 maintained a secret alliance according to the terms of which the Americans treated Sweden on a parity basis with the North Atlantic Treaty Organization (NATO) member states.[9]

To conclude, by the 1970s

> ....there have been, roughly, three periods of post-war Soviet strategy. The first was the initial aftermath of the war when the Soviet Union was in a condition of strategic and economic inferiority. The Soviet Navy was limited to the mission of protecting the flanks of the army and of patrolling Soviet waters and coastlines because of extreme shortages in manpower and in the economy. . . . After 1953, planning for a change in missions was begun. It was based upon the adoption of nuclear power and heavy emphasis on missile warfare. Tactics were developed for moving the defense perimeter further out to sea. The threat from aircraft and naval ballistic missile submarines had led to the need to establish zones of defense further from Moscow, even at the 1,500 kilometer mark, to develop successful antisubmarine warfare and to provide air cover for theaters of action from Soviet air bases.
>
> With the successful development of missiles and rockets – the revolution in military affairs that the Soviets emphasize constantly – they began introducing new tactics for the destruction of Western fleets in specific areas and new strategies for winning, or at least breaking up and neutralizing, the Third World.[10]

Within a Fleet, the vessels were divided into what might best be translated squadrons (*diviziya*, pl. *divizii*; a former term still in occasional use was *eskadra*, pl. *eskadry*), brigades (*brigada*, pl. *brigady*), divisions (*divizion*, pl. *diviziony*), and detachments (*otryad*, pl. *otryady*). A squadron consisted of a large number of vessels of different classes, which were under the same command and expected to operate together. For this reason, the different vessels of the squadron generally had similar characteristics with regard to speed and range. The squadron was commonly subdivided into brigades, each of which consisted of from two to four divisions. A division typically consisted of three or four surface warships of the same, or similar, class, although a submarine division could consist of about 10 submarines. It follows that a division's vessels

Colonel General Sergey Arsent'yevich Gulyayev, commander of Naval Aviation of the Baltic Fleet. (Soviet Ministry of Defence)

also concentrated on one specific mission, such as missile attack or anti-submarine warfare. A section, finally, customarily consisted of a small group of vessels which temporarily operated together, for instance during an exercise.

A Fleet consisted of other organisational components, too. Its integral Naval Aviation component has already been mentioned, but the Navy also included integral Naval Infantry, with each Fleet having an allocated Naval Infantry force of at least regimental strength. Furthermore, the Navy included coastal missile and artillery units in some locations. A Fleet's Naval Bases constituted independent units, as did the various support services, including signals, rescue service, and so on.

The first units which were activated during the crisis engendered by the mutiny on the *Storozhevoy* were, naturally, those of the Navy, specifically those of the Baltic Fleet. We will see that among them, the Naval Aviation units of the Baltic Fleet played a primary role. Since Naval Aviation was fully integrated into the Navy, it follows that individual Naval Aviation units were under the operational control of the Fleet to which they were assigned. Front-line Naval Aviation aircraft included long-range reconnaissance aircraft and heavy long-range bombers armed with air-to-surface missiles (ASM). Naval Aviation bombers carried both nuclear and conventional munitions. Naval Aviation also included a helicopter fleet, primarily employed for anti-submarine warfare, and a few strike aircraft.

It was not only the Navy which was called up to deal with the mutiny within its ranks. Other types of units were raised as well, including those of the KGB Border Troops.

The mission of the Border Troops included traditional border guard tasks. The Border Troops were tasked to prevent illegal border crossings and the illegal transport of weapons, explosives, or contraband across the border. For this reason, they were authorised to monitor the observance of established procedures at border crossing points and examine documents and possessions of persons crossing the borders and to confiscate articles such as contraband but also subversive literature. They also conducted inquiries in cases of violations of the state border, and took such actions as the arrest, search, and interrogation of individuals suspected of border violations. In addition, they monitored the observance by Soviet and foreign ships of navigation procedures in Soviet territorial waters and assisted other state agencies in the preservation of natural resources and the protection of the environment from pollution. However, the mission of the Soviet Border Troops went considerably beyond that of border guards of most other countries. For historical reasons, the Soviet Border Troops were also tasked to repulse armed incursions into the Motherland. This was a commonplace task during the first two decades of the Cold War, when British, American, West German, and Swedish intelligence, as well as a large number of émigré organisations, habitually sent small groups of armed men into Soviet territory for espionage or the provision of clandestine support to the remnants of the once prominent anti-Soviet guerrilla and resistance movements. Anti-Soviet guerrillas had been particularly active in the three Baltic republics, where they were known as Forest Brothers. Most had been eradicated by the 1950s, but in Lithuania, armed resistance of sorts may have lingered on into the early 1970s. The last known fighter, Benediktas Mikulis (1920–2000), emerged as late as in 1971.

At the time of the mutiny on the *Storozhevoy*, the Border Troops administered nine border districts (Russian: *pogranichnyye okruga*, PO) and a few separate border detachments, primarily in the Arctic and at the Moscow airports, which reported directly to the Main Directorate of the Border Troops. Border district boundaries were distinct from civil or military district boundaries, lined up along the nearly 63,000km of the state border under Border Troops' control. The Soviet land border was the longest in the world, so the Border Troops needed a significant number of men. In similarity to the other arms of services, the Border Troops primarily consisted of conscripts drafted as part of the biannual call-up under the direction of the Ministry of Defence. Despite being under the operational control of the KGB, the induction and discharge of Border Troops conscripts were regulated by the 1967 Law on Universal Military Service, which covered all armed forces of the Soviet Union.

The KGB border districts were combined arms formations. They included infantry similar to the army's motor-rifle infantry formed in battalions and companies, but also signals, combat engineers, construction engineers, medical, and supply units, just like those in the Ground Forces. In case of the outbreak of war, the Border Troops were expected to play a very active part in repulsing any enemy invasion.

Soviet Border Troops also included integrated aviation units and maritime border guard units (that is, a coast guard).

Commanded by a major general or a lieutenant general, the Aviation Department of the Border Troops (*Aviatsionnyy otdel Pogranichnykh voysk*) was divided into air regiments, squadrons, and flights, in the same manner as the Air Forces. The chief tasks of the Border Troops aviation units were to deliver supplies and troops to remote border outposts, to deliver foot patrols in remote areas, and under particularly difficult circumstances, to mount helicopter-borne assaults in combat operations. Most of the aircraft were transports, although Border Troops Aviation also included a few Mil Mi-24 attack helicopters.

Those border districts which faced oceans and seas also included units of guard ships (each customarily referred to as a *pogranichnyy storozhevoy korabl'*, PSKR, to distinguish it from the SKR of often the same class which was used by the Navy). The Naval Formations of the Border Troops (*Morskiye chasti Pogranichnykh voysk*) were divided into brigades and divisions just like the Navy. In addition to their patrol tasks, the naval units of the Border Troops also played a substantial role in anti-submarine warfare. The personnel of the Naval Formations of the Border Troops held Navy-style ranks. The Chief of the Naval Directorate within the Main Directorate of the Border Troops was a high-ranking officer, customarily a rear admiral or vice admiral.

The KGB border district which had to deal with the mutiny on the *Storozhevoy* was the Baltic, with headquarters in Riga. This was a recently resurrected border district, which had been re-established as late as on 23 October 1975, only days before the mutiny.

Perhaps unsurprisingly, units of the Air Forces too were called out to deal with the mutiny on the *Storozhevoy*.

The Soviet Air Forces were divided into three branches: Long Range Aviation (Russian: *Dal'naya aviatsiya*), which was tasked with long-range bombardment of strategic targets with nuclear weapons; Frontal (or Tactical) Aviation (*Frontovaya aviatsiya*), whose task it was to support the Ground Forces; and Military Transport Aviation (*Voyenno-transportnaya aviatsiya*), which controlled transport aircraft and provided airlift capability for all requirements of all services. In addition, the civil air fleet, the airline Aeroflot, in times of war and crisis served as an auxiliary service and proved instant back-up when necessary.

Air defence was the responsibility of yet another air organisation, the National Air Defence Forces. Headquartered at Balashikha just outside Moscow, this was the largest air defence force in the world, controlling more than 5,000 early-warning and air search radars, over 2,500 manned interceptors, and some 50,000 surface-to-air missiles (SAM) distributed among over a thousand major missile sites. In case of enemy air attack, the National Air Defence Forces would constitute the final line of defence. However, for obvious reasons this organisation played no significant role in the suppression of the mutiny on the warship *Storozhevoy*.

The *Storozhevoy*

The vigilance and combat readiness of the Soviet armed forces in the Baltic region were severely tested on Saturday 8 November 1975, when a mutiny broke out on the Soviet warship *Storozhevoy* ('Sentry'), which was then temporarily moored in the River Daugava in Riga, the capital of the Soviet Republic of Latvia.

The *Storozhevoy* belonged to a type of warship which in the West then was commonly referred to as a missile destroyer. Armed with surface-to-surface missiles (SSM), the class was known under the NATO-codename 'Krivak'. For some obscure reason, NATO-codenames for Soviet warships were invariably made up to sound Russian even though many, including Krivak, were imaginary words with no meaning in any language.

Riga was a major city on the border with the Western world, so the Soviet military presence was strong, with many army, air force, and naval units based nearby. Many citizens from other parts of the Soviet Union, including officers with their families, gradually settled down in the city. Soviet soldiers and sailors on leave were a common sight. (Medström)

A warship of the class known in the USSR as Project 1135 Burevestnik, and to NATO as the Krivak I – the class to which *Storozhevoy* belonged. The Soviet Navy had the practice of regularly changing hull numbers of its ships, it is therefore unclear if this photograph shows *Storozhevoy* around the time of the mutiny, or sister-ship *Bditelnyy* as of 1971. (US DoD)

Table 1: Technical characteristics of the Storozhevoy at the time of the 1975 mutiny[13]

Displacement	
	Standard: 2,835 tons
	Full load: 3,190 tons
Dimensions	
	Length: 123.0 m
	Beam: 14.2 m
	Draught: 4.28 m
Speed	
	Maximum: 32.2 kts
	Economy: 14 kts
Range	
	4,000 nm (14 kts)
	3,515 nm (18 kts)
	3,155 nm (24 kts)
	1,240 nm (32 kts)
Endurance	
	30 days
Propulsion	
	1x 48,000 hp M7 gas turbine (2x 6,000 hp M60 gas turbines, 2x 18,000 hp M3 boost gas turbines), 2 fixed pitch propellers
Armament	
Anti-submarine warfare (ASW)	1x4 ASW missile launcher type KT-M-1135 URPK-4 Metel' (4x ASW missiles type 85R, each capable of carrying a 5-kt nuclear warhead); SU-85KS-I Musson fire control system
	2x4 533mm ASW positional torpedo tubes type ChTA-53-1135 (4x torpedoes type SET-65, 4x torpedoes type 53-65K); SU-504A Drakon-1135 fire control system
	2x12 ASW rocket depth charge launchers type RBU-6000 Smerch-2 (96x unguided depth charges type RGB-60), with a range of 6,000 m; Burya fire control system
Air defence	2x2 SA missile launchers type ZIF-122 4K33 Osa-M (40x missiles type 9M33); 4R-33 fire control system
	2x2 76mm cannons type AK-726 (1,600-2,000 rounds each); MR-105 Turel' fire control system
Mines	Depending on mission, e.g., 18 mines type IGDM-500; 10 mines type KSMM; 14 mines type KAM; 14 mines type KB Krab; 10 mines type Serpey; 4 mines type PMR-1; 7 mines type PMR-2; 7 mines type MTPK-1; 14 mines type RM-1; or 12 mines type UDM-2
Electronic Warfare (EW)	
	MP-401S Start-S electronic support measures (ESM) system (passive system, based on the interception and identification of enemy electronic emissions)
	PK-16 decoy dispensing system, 4x launchers type KL-101 (128 rounds type AZ-TST-60)
Electronics	
	MR-310A Angara-A air/surface search radar
	Volga navigation radar
	Don-2 navigation radar
	Nickel-KM and Khrom-KM identification Friend/Foe (IFF)
	ARP-50R radio direction finder
	MG-332 Titan-2 hull-mounted sonar

In the 1980s, most Western navies re-designated ships of the Krivak-class as missile frigates, although the Soviets did not change the operational characteristics of the ship class. The Soviets classified the *Storozhevoy* and other vessels of her class as a large anti-submarine warfare ship of the class known as Project 1135 Burevestnik ('Storm petrel'). Beyond this, the *Storozhevoy* was identified by her bow (*bort*) number, which at the time of the mutiny was 500. At regular intervals, the Soviets changed bow numbers of all warships, to make it more difficult for foreign intelligence services to monitor them and their positions.[11]

In war, the *Storozhevoy*'s task was to hunt down enemy submarines, principally those which carried ballistic missiles that posed an immediate threat to the Motherland. The Burevestnik-class of large anti-submarine warfare ships belonged to Gorshkov's anti-submarine warfare programme and was for this reason specifically designed to counter American ballistic missile-armed submarines. In fact, the Burevestnik-class was reputed to be the particular love of Admiral Gorshkov, who wanted a total number of 50 to 60 ships of this class, for deployment in all Soviet fleets (ultimately, 32 units were built).[12] For this purpose, she normally carried an assortment of surface-to-surface missiles designed for anti-submarine warfare, torpedoes, and unguided depth charges. She was also equipped with surface-to-air missiles and automatic cannons for self-defence. The *Storozhevoy* was over 120 metres long, had a displacement of some 3,000 tons, and a crew of almost 200 men (see Table 1). The ship's distinctive features – the bow missile box, the stack, and the angled mast, earned the class a nickname among U. S. sailors derived from their foreign ship

Table 1: Technical characteristics of the Storozhevoy at the time of the 1975 mutiny[13] (*continued*)	
	MG-325 Vega towed array sonar
	MG-26 Khosta underwater communications system
	MGS-400K, KMG-12 Kassandra, MI-110R, MI-110K or MI-110KM, KPF-2-2 sonars
	R-785 Tayfun communications complex
Crew	194 (incl. 29 officers and warrant officers), of whom apparently 142 participated in the mutiny, with the rest being either ashore or locked up (establishment-strength crew for the Burevestnik-class was 197, incl. 23 officers)

silhouette identification training: 'Hot dog pack, smokestack, guns in back – KRIVAK'. Her comprehensive armament made a ship of her class a significant force on the high seas. NATO observers routinely expected her to belong to Baltic Fleet units which in case of war would exit the Baltic to sail out into the Atlantic to hunt for nuclear ballistic missile-armed submarines. Such contingency plans no doubt existed, and vessels of the Burevestnik series occasionally took part in exercises in the northern Atlantic. However, as we have seen, the Baltic Fleet remained primarily focused on territorial defence. The *Storozhevoy* was certainly intended to hunt down enemy submarines, but perhaps no further out than in the northern reaches of the North Sea and perhaps even closer to Soviet borders.

At the time of the mutiny, the *Storozhevoy* carried adequate or full supplies (including of food and water). Her 350 tons of diesel oil gave her an effective maximum range of 1,800 to 1,900 nm (3,500 km), assuming an average speed of 14 kts.[14]

It is frequently claimed that neither missiles, torpedoes, depth charges, nor 76mm rounds were onboard at the time of the mutiny. However, as far as can be ascertained, the *Storozhevoy*, in similarity to other Soviet warships, carried a full weapons-load due to the duty of constant combat readiness. The only exception seems to have been the four ASW missiles type 85R, each capable of carrying a 5-kt nuclear warhead. These missiles seem to have been unloaded in Baltiysk before the *Storozhevoy* set out bound for Riga.[15]

The Burevestnik series was designed as a successor to the class named Project 50 Gornostay, known in the West under NATO-codename Riga. Work on the design began in 1956 and it matured as an anti-submarine ship in the 1960s. The first ship of the series was the *Bditelnyy* ('Vigilant') which was commissioned in 1970. The *Storozhevoy* was the fifth of the series, laid down at the Yantar' Shipyard in Kaliningrad in 1972 and commissioned in December 1973. After final tests she entered service in 1974. At the time of the mutiny, the *Storozhevoy* was an almost new warship.

The *Storozhevoy* had her home port in Baltiysk, near Kaliningrad where the headquarters of the Soviet Baltic Fleet was located. She belonged to the 128th Missile Ship Brigade (Russian: *128-ya brigada raketnykh korabley*, BRK) of the Baltic Fleet.[16] The 128th Missile Ship Brigade was in turn subordinated the 12th Missile Ship Squadron (Russian: *12-ya diviziya raketnykh korablev*) in Baltiysk, commanded by Captain First Rank Valentin Yegorovich Selivanov (b. 1936).[17]

In October 1974, the *Storozhevoy* had sailed to Rostock in East Germany, to celebrate the country's 25th-year anniversary, and then participated in a major naval exercise in the Atlantic Ocean, named Okean-75. She had also visited Cuba in March-April 1975, making a port call in Havana. Then she had returned to the Baltic Sea, where she had participated in additional exercises during October 1975. Already in 1974, she had received a visit from the Soviet Defence Minister, Marshal of the Soviet Union Andrey Grechko, and also been mentioned in several news articles in the Soviet military daily, the *Krasnaya zvezda* ('Red Star').[18] But the attention had not been wholly positive; one of the newspaper articles criticised the officer corps and the Communist Party committee on the *Storozhevoy*, and several officers were mentioned by name, including the commanding officer, Anatoliy Vasil'yevich Potul'nyy (1936–2011), the political officer, Valeriy Mikhaylovich Sablin (1939–1976), and the secretary of the warship's party committee, Vladimir Viktorovich Firsov (b. 1948).[19] Most officers were members of the Communist Party, since this in all but name was a prerequisite for a successful career as a military officer.

The *Storozhevoy* had come to Riga to take part in the celebration of the Day of the Great October Socialist Revolution, which was celebrated in the Soviet Union every year on 7 November to commemorate the October Revolution of 1917. The date was not an anomaly; the October Revolution was so named because Russia then followed the Julian calendar. The Soviet Union adopted the Gregorian calendar in 1921, for which reason the October Revolution henceforth was celebrated as per the revised date, in November, and not in October as before. After participating in a parade of warships during the festivities, the *Storozhevoy* would remain over the weekend in Riga.

2 THE MUTINY

On Saturday 8 November 1975, the *Storozhevoy*'s political officer, Captain Third Rank Valeriy Sablin, set the events in motion that would lead to the mutiny.[1]

As the political officer (*zampolit*), Sablin functioned as the deputy of the ship's commanding officer but with special responsibility for the political education, morale, and spiritual well-being of the crew, who mostly consisted of young conscripts. Invariably a Communist Party member, the political officer was tasked with ensuring that the crew followed socialist dogma as decided by the Party leadership in Moscow. He supervised the Party organisation and conducted Party political work within his unit. The political officer also lectured troops on Marxism-Leninism, the Party's view of international affairs, and the Party's tasks for the armed forces. As the crew's political officer, the thirty-six-year-old Sablin was hardly a man anyone would have expected to mutiny.

Sablin was a convinced communist and was not at all looking for an alternative to the socialist system. Unlikely as it might seem, Sablin's avowed intention was to foment a new communist

Captain Third Rank Valeriy Mikhaylovich Sablin, 'Zampolit' (political officer) of the *Storozhevoy*. (Soviet Ministry of Defence)

Aleksandr Nikolayevich Shein, the conscript sailor who assisted Sablin. (Author's collection)

revolution by taking the warship to Leningrad, where he expected to receive the support of the Navy and the masses. This was also the story that Sablin after the event presented during his court martial. If insufficient support was forthcoming, he may have planned to ask for the support of the United Nations. Sablin certainly included an enigmatic reference to Kurt Waldheim, Secretary-General of the United Nations, in his to-do list. However, the reference does not mention what Sablin had in mind, nor does he seem to have told anybody later.[2]

Sablin believed deeply in socialism. However, he also had a complex and increasingly grandiose personality. In the field of psychology, the term grandiosity refers to an unrealistic sense of superiority, frequently expressed in the overinflation of one's own capability and criticisms of others as inferiors in knowledge and capability. Some of Sablin's colleagues admired him for his apparent sincerity, while others considered him dogmatic and more than a little odd. Sablin had a habit of correcting what he regarded as the mistakes or failings of others. Already in 1961, while still in his early twenties and years before he became a political officer, he wrote a letter to Admiral Grishanov, chief of the Political Directorate of the Navy. In 1963, yet more conspicuously, Sablin wrote and sent a lengthy letter, reportedly dozens of pages, addressed to supreme Soviet leader Nikita Khrushchev, in which he criticised party policies. This was not a smart move in the totalitarian Soviet state and might, under Khrushchev's predecessor Stalin, easily have resulted in a death sentence. Fortunately for Sablin and his family, Khrushchev had abandoned such practices. Yet, the letter resulted in an official KGB investigation of Sablin's activities. Since no harm had been done, he suffered no punishment – except a reprimand by the local party committee. The incident did not affect his naval career, although senior officers certainly were informed about the keen young lieutenant who believed that he knew how to conduct national policy better than the party hierarchy.[3]

Sablin was disappointed with how the Soviet Union had developed. Systemic and structural problems in the central economy and party rule had become increasingly obvious, and reform was necessary. Many others, too, understood the problems and loathed the stagnation that was their result. Defections to the capitalist and freer Western world were not uncommon. But Sablin had a vision of a radically opposite solution to the widespread problems. Through a new socialist revolution, he believed that he would bring the masses together and thereby reform the whole socialist system in the spirit of Marx and Lenin. Ideologically convinced young left-wing radical revolutionaries were commonplace outside the Soviet Union in the 1970s, but Sablin was unique in that he actually became one within the framework of the Soviet Socialist system – and then as its opponent.

Sablin had been dissatisfied with the situation in the Soviet Union for years. However, it was only in April 1975 that he finally decided to act.[4] Since then, he had been preparing tape recordings of the fiery speeches he intended to give to the Soviet people and the telegrams he expected to send to the Politburo in Moscow and other Soviet officials when the revolution began. The problems within the Soviet system were well known to Soviet citizens, but conditions within the armed forces and on Soviet warships were particularly difficult, and especially so for new conscripts. The crew on the *Storozhevoy*, as on other ships, were often dissatisfied with the living conditions on board. Sablin was well aware of this. In his role as a political officer, he had good contact with large sections of the crew, and unlike many other political officers, Sablin was by all accounts genuinely popular with the sailors. He took advantage of this when planning the mutiny. On 5 November 1975, immediately after leaving Baltiysk on the way to Riga, Sablin persuaded a young rating named Aleksandr Nikolayevich Shein (b. 1955) to help him in the coming mutiny. The 20-year-old Seaman Shein, who like Sablin had been a year on the *Storozhevoy* and looked up to his political officer (both belonged to the ship's original crew), then recruited a few more co-conspirators among friends within the crew. Before conscription, Shein had dropped out of school. He had also been caught stealing state property shortly before conscription. However, he was a good mechanic and had a talent for art.[5]

All ships in the Soviet Navy were manned by conscripted junior ratings and the *Storozhevoy* was no exception. Conscripts came from throughout the Soviet Union. Crewmen of 18 nationalities served onboard the *Storozhevoy*. The crew was broadly representative of the Soviet population as a whole. The majority, 111 of 194, were

A rear view of the *Storozhevoy*, seen in 1975, before the mutiny. (Author's Collection)

ethnic Russians, and the crew also included 22 Ukrainians and 12 Belarusians, which roughly corresponded to the size of these respective Soviet republics. However, crewmen from other parts of the vast Soviet territory served on the *Storozhevoy*, too, including from Muslim regions of the Caucasus or Central Asia.

Conscripted usually at age 18, the ratings first went through six months of training, after which they served for two and a half years with the fleet. A new intake of conscripts took place twice a year, so it was customary for a crew to be in a continual state of flux. Although most left after their mandatory time of service, at age 21, a rating could then volunteer to sign on as a petty officer. But such men constituted the minority. This, together with the continual state of flux within the crew, meant that experienced and assertive conscripts such as Shein acquired considerable influence with the younger conscripts.

Sablin chose the date of the mutiny with care. On the afternoon of Saturday 8 November 1975, when Sablin set his plan in motion, the Soviet Navy had just celebrated the anniversary of the Russian Revolution. This was symbolically important, because Sablin by this choice was able to link his mutiny to the historic October Revolution. The evening in question was also very suitable for a mutiny, as a large part of the Soviet military was on leave or celebrating, usually with strong drinks. But there was another reason, and that was probably the decisive factor. Sablin had had just over a year to get to know the crew and the ship. But immediately after the celebration in Riga, the *Storozhevoy* would go to Liepaja (now Liepāja) to get a new crew there and to be prepared for transfer to the Pacific Fleet.

Key people in the new crew had already arrived in Liepaja.[6] For Sablin, it was now or never. The opportunity to mutiny might never come again. On Friday 7 November 1975, the day before he set his plan in motion, Sablin wrote in his diary: 'Sometimes you wait almost half your life for your one moment to come.'[7] Sablin now reckoned that his one moment finally had arrived. He wrote a letter to his parents, informing them that he planned to do something radical. The letter reached them five days later. Sablin had planned it this way, so that they would be unable to stop him. Earlier, he had sent an even more vague hint of what he intended to do to his wife Nina. In this letter, posted in Baltiysk before the *Storozhevoy* set out bound for Riga, Sablin merely explained that he would take 'the path of revolutionary struggle', an expression commonplace in Marxism-Leninism. This letter reached Nina on the same day as Sablin carried out his plan, and she would only find out that something serious had happened by hearsay, on the following day.[8]

Sablin did not post the letter to his parents himself. Instead, for unclear reasons, he on 7 November sent Shein ashore to post the letter. But Sablin also gave Shein a few other tasks, as part of the conspiracy to seize the *Storozhevoy*. Sablin had recorded three copies of the speeches and telegrams that he would broadcast from the *Storozhevoy*, after the mutiny had taken place. Perhaps to assure himself of a larger audience if something went wrong, he now gave Shein one of the tapes in a cardboard box, with instructions to find somebody trustworthy who could post it to a former member of the *Storozhevoy*'s crew, who had remained in Baltiysk. Sablin hoped that this man then would make sure that the messages reached the public, in case his plan failed. But who could be entrusted with the critical task of posting the package? Sablin had not thought this through, he merely instructed Shein to locate a trustworthy person in Riga, and then ask this person to post the tape to the addressee later. Shein did as best as he could; he approached a group of girl students on the street, picked up a conversation with one of them, and finally gave her the package with the tape recording, asking her to post it (the girl

Poor but unique photograph showing the *Storozhevoy* in 1974, before the voyage to Cuba. (Author's Collection)

either did not have time to post the package, or possibly forgot all about it, so it remained in her possession throughout the mutiny).[9]

As for Sablin, he too left the ship on the evening of 7 November. He spent almost three hours away from the *Storozhevoy*. It remains unknown what he did. He had apparently already handed over the conspiratorial work, such as it was, to Shein. According to Sablin's own testimony, he merely took a walk, sat down for a while in a café, and then took the last cutter back to the *Storozhevoy*, together with those sailors who returned from shore leave.[10]

On the following night (that is, Saturday), Sablin began the realisation of the ambitious plan. As a political officer, it was part of his job to show politically appropriate films for the crew. This evening he chose to show Sergey Eisenstein's great film *Battleship Potemkin* from 1925, which was about a mutiny on a Russian ship in connection with the revolution of 1905. That film was not only ideologically appropriate; it also showed how Sablin predicted the outcome of the mutiny. In the film, the Tsarist fleet gathers to stop the bold mutineers on the *Potemkin*, but when it comes down to it, the honest sailors on the Tsarist ships refuse to open fire at the mutineers. In the film, the *Potemkin* continues right through the Tsarist fleet, in the direction of freedom and revolution, without being attacked by the lackeys of imperialism.

The mutineers struck soon after 7:00 p.m., when a third of the crew was on shore leave.[11] The last entry in the *Storozhevoy*'s log was entered at 7:00 p.m., when a new duty officer signed in – one of those who supported Sablin.[12] Within minutes, Sablin and Shein surprised and locked up the ship's commanding officer, Captain Second Rank Anatoliy Potul'nyy, in an isolated area.[13] Subsequently, Sablin, in his capacity as the senior officer present on board, summoned the remaining officers to a meeting at 7:30 p.m. While the film about the mutiny on the *Battleship Potemkin* kept the rest of the crew occupied (there had already been a first film show during the afternoon, but possibly of another film), Sablin said that he had detained the warship's commanding officer, explained the situation, and asked for the officers' support for the revolution. Meanwhile, Shein monitored the meeting from the outside, armed with Sablin's pistol, ready to intervene if necessary. During the meeting, Sablin said that he intended to sail to Leningrad to start the revolution there. He also explained that the sailors in Leningrad were on their side, something that lacked any ground in reality, but none of those

Vladimir Viktorovich Firsov, officer in charge of the *Storozhevoy*'s electronics and chairman of the party committee. (Author's Collection)

present could know this. Some declared themselves willing to help, and the others were locked up.

At 10:10 p.m., Sablin called the entire crew to a meeting. Most had returned from shore leave. It had now dawned on everyone that the captain had been locked up and the mutiny was a fact. Sablin gave another speech in which he said that they would sail to Leningrad to explain the situation to the people. He also said that many officers in Leningrad, the Northern Fleet, and the Pacific Fleet were on their side, just waiting for the *Storozhevoy* to hoist the banner of the revolution. Sablin was a skilled speaker, and he brought the crew with him. But not everyone. Two loyal petty officers, Kopylov and Nabiyev, made an awkward attempt to stop Sablin and free the captain, but they were quickly thwarted. Most of the crew chose not to oppose the mutiny, either because they supported Sablin or because they did not dare. Although both petty officers, warrant officers, and officers were drawn from volunteers, the former were little more than experienced conscripts, while most officers were technical specialists. Officer training emphasised technical subjects. With the major share of the crew consisting of conscripts, the operation of a ship depended on the expertise provided by the professional officers. Most officers expected to remain technical specialists for the duration of their career. For this reason, most officers, too, hesitated to confront Sablin, who after all was the senior officer present.

However, one of those who had initially said that he was willing to support Sablin, the aforementioned Senior Lieutenant Vladimir Firsov, in charge of a section of the ship's electronics as well as chairman of the party committee onboard the warship, decided to leave the ship to sound the alarm. After or during Sablin's meeting with the crew, apparently at or around 10:30 p.m., Senior Lieutenant Bulat Talipovich Saitov (b. 1947), another loyalist, assisted Firsov in climbing down from the deck of the ship to the buoy at which the *Storozhevoy* was moored. From there, Firsov managed to get the attention of somebody, apparently a sentry, on the quay next to a nearby submarine, the S-263. After some confusion, the submariners sent a cutter to retrieve Firsov from the buoy. Upon arrival, he alerted the submarine's commanding officer, Captain Second Rank L. Svetlovskiy, who in addition to being commanding officer of the submarine also temporarily served as roadstead duty officer for the ships on the River Daugava. This made him responsible for any sudden emergency among the ships at anchor there. Surely, a mutiny would have qualified as an emergency. However, at first Svetlovskiy did not believe Firsov's tale of a mutiny on the *Storozhevoy*.[14] The story sounded insane and was simply too improbable.

3
THE PURSUIT

When Sablin found out that Firsov had skipped out, he realised that they could not wait any longer. Sablin understood, now, if not earlier, that it was impossible to go directly to Leningrad. The shortest route was through the Moon Sound, which connects the Gulf of Riga with the Gulf of Finland. Presumably, Sablin had stated his intention to use this route to Leningrad. However, the Moon Sound is difficult to navigate for large vessels, requires pilots, and is easily blocked. Sablin therefore intended to take the *Storozhevoy* out to international waters, from where he could broadcast his recorded radio speech to the Soviet people, and if it did not lead to revolution, perhaps appeal to the United Nations for help.

Sablin began preparing the *Storozhevoy* for departure at about 1:00 a.m.[1] This took time, not least because Sablin also had to confront an attempt by the aforementioned Senior Lieutenant Saitov and a few other officers and warrant officers to stop the mutiny and arrest him. Saitov and his friends had access to pistols. However, none of the officers was willing actually to use deadly force against their colleagues, so ultimately Sablin and his supporters among the sailors prevailed. The loyalists were locked up with the others.[2]

As a result of these delays, the *Storozhevoy* did not leave Riga until about 2:15 a.m. Around 2:50 a.m. she moved out into the Gulf of Riga.[3] Sablin set a course for the Baltic Sea, heading west with a speed of just over 15 knots in the direction of the Irben Sound, which leads out into the Baltic Sea. Sablin did not want to be noticed, so the *Storozhevoy* proceeded without turning on either her air/surface search radar or her navigation radar. For this reason she could not move very fast in the darkness.

By then, Firsov was already attempting to explain the situation to those in charge of base security. It was not only the roadstead duty officer, Svetlovskiy, who found it hard to believe his story. Firsov also had to tell his tale to the chief of staff for the 78th Ship Security Brigade for the protection of the water area (Russian: *78-ya brigada korabley okhrany*), Captain Second Rank V. S. Vlasov, and the head of the Brigade Special Detachment (Russian: *osobyy otdel brigady*), Captain Second Rank V. G. Yudin. They were in charge of the Ust'-Dvinsk neighbourhood in northwestern Riga on the left bank of the River Daugava (the neighbourhood is currently known as Daugavgrīva). Just as Svetlovskiy before them, Vlasov and Yudin found the story hard to credit. While they several times did attempt to contact the *Storozhevoy* by radio, nobody onboard responded (Sablin had told them not to). Finally, after having vacillated for several hours and growing increasingly worried, Vlasov and Yudin armed themselves with pistols, rounded up three sailors with assault rifles from the guard post, and then brought Firsov along in a cutter to board the *Storozhevoy* to clarify what was happening there. They were too late. By then, the *Storozhevoy* had already left the anchorage and was heading out towards the Bay of Riga.[4]

Having convinced themselves that Firsov told the truth, Vlasov and Yudin finally contacted the command post of the Baltic Fleet. After the Day of the Great October Socialist Revolution, as after other national holidays, a significant share of Soviet military personnel traditionally was knocked out by vodka consumption in connection with the celebration. For this reason, usually no extensive military activity was carried out on such a day. But the military command posts still maintained combat readiness, and now they reacted relatively quickly, despite any previous celebration. Somebody awakened the commanding officer of the Baltic Fleet, Vice Admiral Anatoliy Mikhaylovich Kosov (1927–1995). An old hand who previously had commanded a nuclear submarine and until recently had been the chief of staff of the Baltic Fleet, Kosov reacted much faster than the overly cautious Svetlovskiy, Vlasov, and Yudin. He ordered that warships immediately set out in pursuit of the *Storozhevoy*. Within 45 minutes of the *Storozhevoy*'s departure,

Vice Admiral Anatoliy Mikhaylovich Kosov, commanding officer of the Baltic Fleet. (Author's collection)

A warship of the class known in the USSR as Project 50 Gornostay (ASCC/NATO-codename 'Riga'). (Photo: U.S. Department of Defense)

at 3:00 a.m., the first warship left Riga in pursuit: an apparently never named patrol ship known to the Baltic Fleet only as SKR-14.

Based on Firsov's testimony, Kosov and his staff probably suspected that the mutineers intended to go directly to Leningrad, through the difficult-to-navigate Moon Sound in the Soviet Republic of Estonia. Having sounded the alarm in Riga, Kosov immediately alerted Tallinn Naval Base, at the Estonian capital. At the same time, as we have seen, the aforementioned patrol ship SKR-14 set out from Riga with orders to intercept and capture the *Storozhevoy*.[5] SKR-14 belonged to the class called Project 50 Gornostay ('ermine'), known to NATO under the reporting name RIGA. Being unnamed, she was otherwise identified only by the bow number, which at the time was 620. This class of warship, smaller and of an older generation than the *Storozhevoy*, was designed for anti-submarine warfare. Kosov also tried, with a first attempt shortly after the departure of the SKR-14, to reach radio contact with the *Storozhevoy*. These attempts were repeated during the night and in the morning, but as far as is known the *Storozhevoy* did not acknowledge these messages, at least not until later. Kosov also certainly contacted the headquarters of the Commander-in-Chief of the Soviet Navy, Admiral of the Fleet of the Soviet Union Sergey Gorshkov, who was in Moscow.

At around 4:30 a.m., Kosov ordered a large interception force consisting of a number of warships out to sea from Liepaja Naval Base, further south. It was commanded by Captain First Rank

A warship of the class known as Project 204 (ASCC/NATO-codename 'Poti'). (Photo: U.S. Department of Defense)

Table 2: Technical characteristics of the *Komsomolets Litvy* at the time of the 1975 mutiny[6]	
Displacement	
	Standard: 1,054 tons
	Full load: 1,186 tons
Dimensions	
	Length: 96.6 m
	Beam: 10.2 m
	Draft: 2.9 m
Speed	
	Maximum: 29.5 kts
	Economy: 15.1 kts
Range	
	1,950 nm (15.1 kts)
	2,200 nm (14.5 kts)
Endurance	
	5 days
Propulsion	
	2x 10,000 hp TV-9 steam turbines
Armament	
	3x1 100mm cannons type B-34USMA (660 rounds); Sfera-50 with radar Yakor'-M fire control system
	2x2 37mm anti-aircraft machine guns type V-11M (4,500 rounds)
	1x3 533mm positional torpedo tubes type TTA-53-50 (3x torpedoes type SET-65)
	2x16 ASW rocket depth charge launchers type RBU-2500 Smerch (128x unguided depth charges type RGB-25), with a range of 2,500 m; Deviz fire control system
	4x mortars type BMB-2 (36x unguided depth charges type BPS)
Electronic Warfare (EW)	
	Bizan'-4 electronic support measures (ESM) system
	BOKA-DU towed decoy system
Electronics	
	Planshet-50 Naval Tactical Data System (BIUS)
	Fut-N air/surface search radar
	Neptun-M surface search radar
	Don navigation radar
	Pegas-3M sonar
	MG-16 Sviyaga underwater communication system
Crew	
	168 (including 11 officers)

Leonid Semyonovich Rassukovannyy (b. 1938), who led the force aboard the patrol ship *Komsomolets Litvy*, the duty ship, which two hours later, at 6:28 a.m., departed from Liepaja at high speed, about 25 knots which was close to her maximum.

The *Komsomolets Litvy* ('Young Communist of Lithuania') belonged to the same ship class as the SKR-14: the Project 50 Gornostay class (ASCC/NATO-codename 'Riga'). A ship of this class was designated a patrol ship (*storozhevoy korabl'*, SKR). We will see that this class designation, identical to the name of the *Storozhevoy*, later produced some confusion. At the time of the mutiny, she carried the bow number 624. The *Komsomolets Litvy* belonged to the 76th Destroyer Brigade (Russian: *76-ya brigada eskadrennykh minonostsev, BEM*), which Rassukovannyy commanded himself. The 76th Destroyer Brigade, a somewhat archaic name within the Soviet Navy, was in turn subordinated Valentin Selivanov's 12th Missile Ship Squadron in Baltiysk, that is, the same squadron to which also the *Storozhevoy* belonged.

The *Komsomolets Litvy* was smaller, older, and slightly slower than the *Storozhevoy* (Table 2). She was built in Kaliningrad Yantar' Shipyard (No. 820) in 1956 and commissioned in the same year. She was known as the *Komsomolets Lity* from October 1962 onwards.

Rassukovannyy and Sablin knew each other, but they were apparently not friends. Rassukovannyy had until recently commanded the 128th Missile Ship Brigade, to which the *Storozhevoy* belonged. Sablin had then served under him. However, their mutual antagonism reportedly went back to their Naval Academy days. Sablin had graduated one year before Rassukovannyy. For this reason, Sablin considered himself of equal status vis-à-vis his commanding officer and, moreover, regarded himself as the more experienced officer. For obvious reasons, this attitude had not endeared Sablin to Rasukovannyy.[7]

Rassukovannyy's patrol ship *Komsomolets Litvy* was soon followed by three subordinate small anti-submarine warfare ships (*malyy protivolodochnyy korabl'*, MPK), identified by their bow numbers 121, 141 and 146, of the Project 204 class under the command of Captain Second Rank Aleksandr V. Bobrakov.[8] Western navies generally referred to them as missile corvettes, with the NATO-codename 'Poti'. The class, an old design from 1956 (the first units of the class were commissioned in 1960), was exclusively intended for anti-submarine warfare. The design was the first major type of Soviet warship to incorporate gas turbines. However, it was also the fastest class of anti-submarine warfare ships constructed

Table 3: Technical characteristics of the Project 204 class small anti-submarine warfare ships at the time of the 1975 mutiny[9]

Displacement	
	Standard: 439 tons
	Full load: 555 tons
Dimensions	
	Length: 58.64 m
	Beam: 8.13 m
	Draft: 3.09 m
Speed	
	Maximum: 35 kts
	Economy: 14 kts
Range	
	2,650 nm (13.75 kts)
	2,500 nm (14 kts)
	1,500 nm (17.68 kts)
	350 nm (33 kts)
Endurance	
	7 days
Propulsion	
	2x 15,000 hp D-2B gas turbines, 2x 4,750 hp M-504A diesels, 2 fixed pitch propellers
Armament	4x1 400mm ASW torpedo tubes type OTA-40-204 (4x torpedoes type SET-40); Zummer fire control system
	2x12 ASW rocket depth charge launchers type RBU-6000 Smerch-2 (96x unguided depth charges type RGB-60), with a range of 6,000 m; Tyulpan fire control system
	1x2 57mm dual-purpose guns type AK-725 (1,100 rounds); MR-103 Bars fire control system
Electronic Warfare (EW)	
	Bizan'-4B electronic support measures (ESM) system
Electronics	
	MR-302 Rubka air/surface search radar
	Donets or Vaygach navigation radar
	Nichrom-M identification Friend/Foe (IFF)
	ARP-50 radio direction finder
	MG-312 Titan-2 or GS-572 Gerkules-2M sonar
Crew	
	54-55 (including 5 officers)

in the Soviet Union, with a maximum speed higher than that of the far more modern but significantly larger *Storozhevoy*. The two propellers were mounted in thrust tubes which extended their length. Moreover, the gas turbines were used to power air compressors which exhausted into the thrust tubes to create extra thrust. The prominent air intakes in the raised stern section gave the ship a distinctive appearance (see Table 3).

But there were already other armed vessels between the *Storozhevoy* and international waters. In the Soviet Union, it was the Border Troops, which belonged to the security service KGB, which was responsible for preventing citizens from fleeing the country. Several fast torpedo vessels from the Border Troops, of the Soviet designation Project 205P Tarantul ('tarantula'), awaited the *Storozhevoy*'s arrival at the Irben Sound. The Border Troops classified the type as a border guard ship (*pogranichnyy storozhevoy korabl'*, PSKR). Western navies referred to the class along its NATO-codename 'Stenka', and commonly called them patrol boats. They were 40-metre-long vessels armed with guns and torpedoes guarding the territorial waters of the Soviet Union (see Table 4). The first was built in Leningrad in 1967. The force, already in the Irben Sound and a part of the 4th Independent Border Guard Ship Brigade (Russian: *4-ya otdel'naya brigada pogranichnykh storozhevykh korabley, OBrPSK*) in Liepaja, was led by Captain Second Rank Aleksey S. Neypert. These patrol vessels discovered the *Storozhevoy* at 7:43 a.m. Neypert repeatedly attempted to communicate with the *Storozhevoy* by semaphore, ordering her to stop and cast anchor, but Sablin refused to comply.[10] The Border Troops had a chain of command separate from that of the Navy. When Neypert reached the *Storozhevoy*, he was ordered to open fire and sink her. Neypert may well have hesitated to do so, but in any case, the order was rescinded before he could carry it out. The reason was probably that within minutes of his detecting the *Storozhevoy*, Moscow suddenly altered the chain of command to deal with the extraordinary situation (the details of which will be described below). The *Storozhevoy* accordingly continued on her way through the Irben Sound, but henceforth accompanied by Neypert's contingent, which continued the attempts to signal her, by radio, semaphore, and loudspeakers.[11]

The Revolutionary Committee

By this time, communications of sorts had already been established between Sablin and Vice Admiral Kosov, the commanding officer of the Baltic Fleet. Since at least 3:25 a.m., Kosov's command post had attempted to contact the *Storozhevoy* by encrypted telegram as a means to discover what was going on. At first, Sablin ordered Yefremov, the ship's radioman, not to respond to any message from

A Border Guard ship of the class known as Project 205P Tarantul (ASCC/NATO-codename 'Stenka'). Thirty were built in Leningrad and in Vladivostok as gunboats and patrol boats for Border Guards, while another 30 served in the Black Sea. (Photo by A. G. Kuzenkov)

naval command. At around 4:00 a.m., Sablin gave Yefremov a telegram which he had already prepared, instructing the radioman to send it straight to the Commander-in-Chief of the Soviet Navy, Admiral Gorshkov. Having encrypted the telegram, Yefremov sent it at 4:22 a.m. In the telegram, marked Secret (*sekretno*) and addressed to the Commander-in-Chief of the Soviet Navy, Sablin presented the demands from the *Storozhevoy*. Ultimately, he wanted the Navy to forward his demands straight to the General Secretary of the Communist Party and thus the Soviet Union's supreme leader, Leonid Ilyich Brezhnev (1906–1982). In 1964, Brezhnev had amassed sufficient power and support to outmanoeuvre and replace Khrushchev and he had retained this powerful position ever since. Khrushchev was by no means a radical, but even so, Brezhnev was unsympathetic to his predecessor's attempts at political reform, however inadequate they may have been. Moreover, Brezhnev was careful to minimise dissent within the party top leadership by making sure that any decision reached was by consensus. Unfortunately, Brezhnev's insistence on consensus engendered pervasive corruption, falling economic growth, stagnation, and many of those societal ills that had provoked Sablin into his mutiny and attempted revolution.

Presumably well-aware of this, Sablin wrote:

> Please immediately bring to the attention of the Politburo and personally to L. I. Brezhnev.
>
> Our demands:
>
> 1. We declare that the territory of our ship is a free territory and independent of state and party institutions until 1 May 1976.
>
> 2. To provide an opportunity to allow one member of the crew, of our choosing, to go on state radio and television for thirty minutes from 9.30 p.m. until 10.00 p.m. Moscow time every day, beginning from the appointed time.
>
> 3. The provision to the ship of all kinds of food supplies, according to present norms, in any naval base.
>
> 4. To allow the *Storozhevoy* an anchorage and mooring buoy in any port in Soviet territorial waters.

Sablin (second from right) with three crewmembers of *Storozhevoy*. (Author's Collection)

Table 4: Technical characteristics of the Project 205P Tarantul border guard ships at the time of the 1975 mutiny[12]	
Displacement	
	Standard: 211 tons
	Full load: 245 tons
Dimensions	
	Length: 39.8 m
	Beam: 7.9 m
	Draft: 1.96 m
Speed	
	Maximum: 34 kts
	Economy: 14 kts
Range	
	1,500 nm (11.5 kts)
	800 nm (20 kts)
	500 nm (35 kts)
Endurance	
	10 days
Propulsion	
	3x 4,000 hp M-503G diesels, 3 propellers
Armament	
	2x2 30mm guns type AK-230; SU MR-104 Rys' fire control system
	4x1 400mm ASW torpedo tubes (4x torpedoes type SET-40)
	2x depth charge racks type BSU-6 (12x unguided depth charges type BB-1)
Electronics	
	4Ts-30-125 radar
	Ksenon radar
	MG-329 Sheksna sonar
	MG-11 Tamir-11 sonar
Crew	
	31 (including 5 officers, 4 warrant officers)

5. To secure mail delivery to the *Storozhevoy*.

6. To allow broadcasts from the *Storozhevoy*'s radio station on the Radio Mayak [public radio] network in the evenings.

7. To allow members of our crew ashore under conditions of immunity.

8. To use no kind of violence or coercion against the families, parents, and close ones of our crewmen.

Our action is purely political in character and is in no way a betrayal of the Motherland, and in case of military operations we are ready to serve in the first line of defenders of the Motherland. Those who will act against us betray the Motherland.

During the next six hours, beginning from 4:00 a.m., the members of the Revolutionary Committee will await the political response to our demands.

In case of silence or if our demands are rejected, or if attempts are made to use force against us, all responsibility for what follows will lay with the Politburo of the Central Committee of the Communist Party of the Soviet Union and personally with L. I. Brezhnev.

[Signed by] the members of the ship's Revolutionary Committee and Captain Third Rank Sablin[13]

The telegram had been ready since April, when Sablin first drafted and then also recorded it on audio tape. Now, he finally got the chance to send it. And as for the one man of their choosing to appear on television, Sablin almost certainly had already selected himself.[14]

The Revolutionary Committee? What had happened onboard the *Storozhevoy*, and when was this committee, by Sablin abbreviated *Revkom* in the Leninist manner, formed? The reality was that no such committee had been formed, except in Sablin's imagination. He had merely made up the name so that his announcement and, of course, the mutiny itself would appear more convincing and give the impression and authority of a solid political movement.[15]

Unfortunately for Sablin, his encrypted telegram did not elicit the response he had hoped for, and possibly even expected. Instead, new and increasingly urgent messages followed from Kosov's command post in Baltiysk. Essentially, the Navy ordered the *Storozhevoy* to cast anchor, cease operations, and then return to port. Nothing was mentioned with regard to Sablin's demands. And Sablin, in the same spirit, refused to respond to the repeated orders to cast anchor.

At around 6:00 a.m., Sablin was tired of the urgent messages from Kosov's command post in Baltiysk. It was time to broadcast the message about the open declaration of mutiny which he also had prepared in April. Sablin instructed Yefremov to broadcast the declaration on an open channel so that everybody within range would hear it. This message would initiate the revolution that Sablin expected to follow from his actions.

Sablin (left) with his commanding officer, Anatoliy Vasil'yevich Potul'nyy. (Author's Collection)

To all! To all! To all!

This is the large anti-submarine warfare ship *Storozhevoy*. We turned through the commander of the navy to the Central Committee of the Communist Party of the Soviet Union and the Soviet government with our demand to provide an opportunity for one of our crewmen to appear on state radio and television to present to the Soviet people our aims and the tasks of our political announcement.

We are neither traitors to the Motherland nor fortune-seekers seeking fame by any means. There is an extreme but necessary opportunity openly to address a range of questions about the political, social, and economic development of our country, about the future of our people, requiring collective, namely, nationwide discussion without pressure from government or party organs. We decided to make this announcement with a clear understanding of our responsibility for the fate of the Motherland, and with a feeling of burning desire to attain real, open relations with our society. But we also recognize the danger of being destroyed physically or morally at the hands of state organs or hired goons. Therefore, we look for support from all honest people in our country and abroad. And, if at the time appointed by us, today at 9:30 p.m. Moscow time, a representative from our ship does not appear on your television screens, we ask you not to go to work the next day and continue this television strike until the government ceases its harsh repression of freedom of speech and until our meeting with you takes place. Support us, comrades! Goodbye until next time.[16]

Leonid Ilyich Brezhnev (seated), supreme leader of the Soviet Union, and Yuriy Vladimirovich Andropov (standing), Chairman of the KGB. (Medström)

Yefremov sent the message, but unknown to Sablin, he did not broadcast it on an open channel. Instead, he used the closed naval communications channel which he had used previously. He later explained his use of a closed channel with the words that an open broadcast was against naval regulations.[17] As a result, Sablin's message never reached the wide audience he had hoped for.

'Bomb the ship and sink it!'

Meanwhile, serious decisions were taken in Moscow. Having learned of the mutiny, Vice Admiral Kosov had immediately contacted Admiral Gorshkov, who was asleep in his villa outside Moscow. Reportedly at around 4:15 a.m., Gorshkov, in turn, informed the Minister of Defence, Marshal Grechko. As a result, Grechko in his turn woke up the Soviet Union's supreme leader Brezhnev early in the morning to inform him of the mutiny.

Although Brezhnev was a cautious ruler who preferred to minimise dissent within the party top leadership by making sure that any decision reached was by consensus, he could act decisively when necessary, as was evident in the manner in which he ousted Krushchev. Now, apparently at about 6:00 a.m. during this early Sunday morning, Brezhnev's immediate response to the *Storozhevoy* crisis was clear and could not be misinterpreted. Soon after, Grechko reportedly informed Gorshkov that Brezhnev had personally ordered him to 'bomb the ship and sink it!'[18] In short, Moscow could not allow the *Storozhevoy* and all her military technology to fall into

Four officers from the *Storozhevoy* during shore leave in March 1975 in Varadero beach resort, Cuba, with V. Firsov in foreground. (Author's Collection)

enemy hands. The ship must be sunk rather than allowed to escape. As the head of the Navy, Gorshkov had to stop the *Storozhevoy* by any available means. For this reason, he was now given command of the Border Troops vessels in the area of operations in addition to those of the Navy, which he already controlled.

There is some uncertainty over exactly when Brezhnev gave the order, because years later the participants in the incident retold the events differently. The Soviet leadership likely hoped that the mutineers would regain their senses and surrender, but they surely also wanted the option to employ deadly force, if this became necessary. It is certain that naval and air units involved in the suppression of the mutiny early on received orders to prepare for the option to sink the *Storozhevoy*. Losing the *Storozhevoy* to the enemy in the West was simply out of the question. The top government would rather use deadly force.[19]

As a result, apparently about 7:45 a.m., Admiral Gorshkov assumed personal command of the operation to intercept and regain control over the *Storozhevoy*. With this alteration in the chain of command, unprecedented in peacetime, even Neypert's patrol vessels were henceforth subordinated Gorshkov's Navy headquarters in Moscow.

Unsurprisingly, everybody assumed that the *Storozhevoy*'s crew intended to flee to Sweden to seek political asylum there. This was bad enough in itself, but even worse would be to lose to the Western powers a completely new warship, full of up-to-date weaponry, electronics, cipher systems, and all sorts of military secrets on board. Nobody in the Soviet leadership doubted that if a ship mutinied and

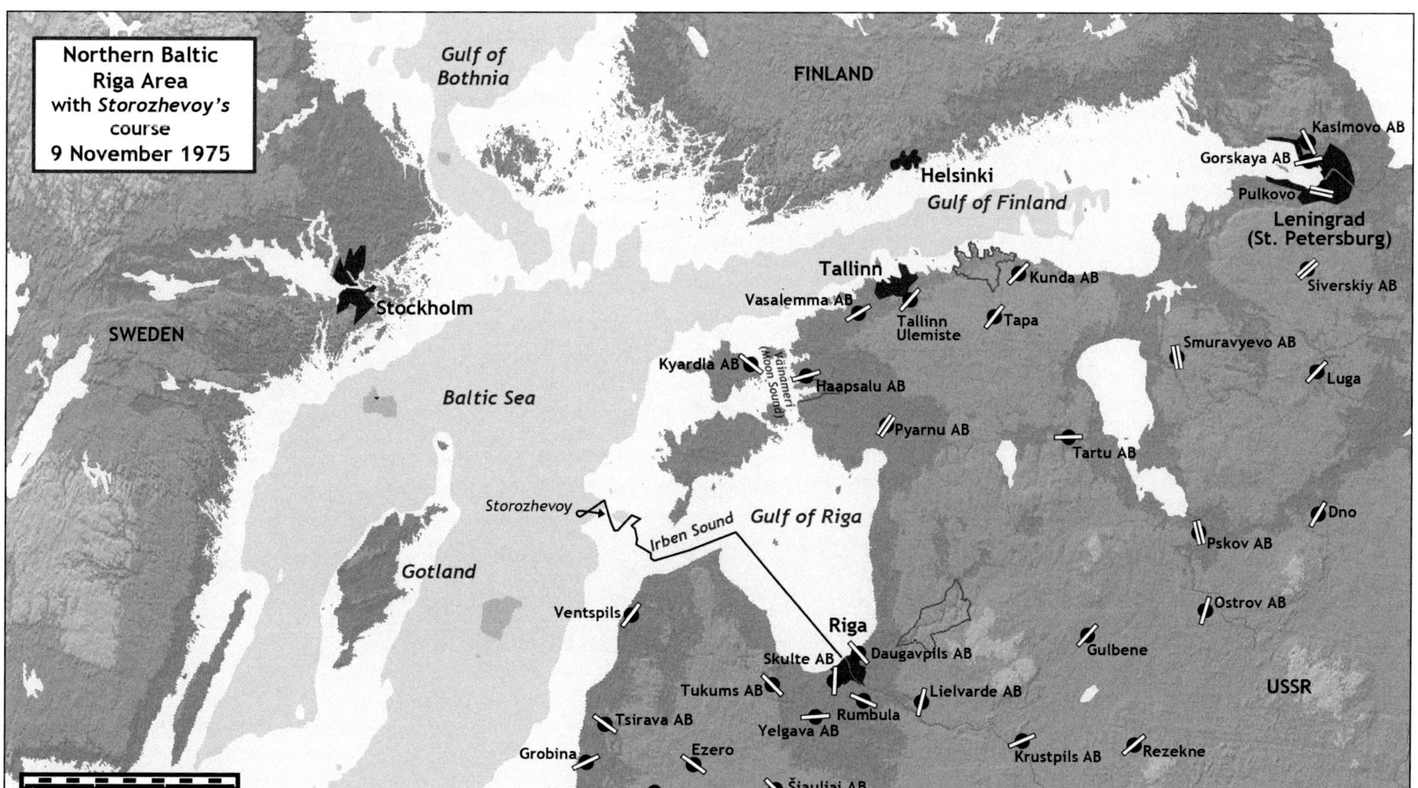

The Riga area, with the nearest military air bases and *Storozhevoy*'s movments during the mutiny. (Map by Tom Cooper)

set course for Sweden, the crew's primary motivation was to flee the Motherland. Political defections from the socialist camp were common, and events of this kind had occurred. In 1952, the Polish survey vessel HG 11 had been taken over by mutineers outside the port-town of Kołobrzeg. These had immediately set course for the Swedish port of Ystad. Going into port there, more than half the crew immediately chose to stay in Sweden.[20] Even in the Soviet Navy, mutinies had taken place. In 1961, a Soviet naval officer of Lithuanian origin named Jonas Pleškys, by manipulating the compass, took his ship to the Swedish island of Gotland, where he sought political asylum. He then settled in the United States.[21] That the mutiny on the *Storozhevoy* could be due to an idealistic left-wing revolutionary whose sole purpose was to start a socialist revolution was an idea that went against all logic and common sense, at least for the Soviet leadership.

4
NAVAL AVIATION TAKES ACTION

In the morning, air assets also began to take part in the action. First one, then another Ilyushin Il-38 maritime patrol and anti-submarine warfare (ASW) aircraft were sent up to search for the *Storozhevoy*. The Il-38 was a modern four-engine aircraft that first came into service in 1970. It was known in the West under the NATO-codename 'May'. The two aircraft belonged to the Baltic Fleet's 145th Independent Anti-Submarine Warfare Aviation Squadron (Russian: *145-ya otdel'naya protivolodochnaya aviatsionnaya eskadril'ya, OPLAE*), based at the Riga Skulte Air Base. The first reconnaissance aircraft, under the command of Captain Anatoliy Grishkin, was in the air before 7:45 a.m. – at about the same time as Captain Neypert's patrol vessels discovered the *Storozhevoy* – and Grishkin's crew located the *Storozhevoy* for the first time at around 8:05 a.m., when she was on her way through the Irben Sound. Until 1972, when the Anti-Submarine Warfare Aviation Squadron received its Il-38 aircraft and thus also partly new personnel, Captain Grishkin belonged to the 170th Guard Smolensk Red Banner Missile Bomber Naval Aviation Regiment (Russian: *170-y gvardeyskiy Smolenskiy Krasnoznamyonnyy morskoy raketonosnyy aviatsionnyy polk, GvMRAP*) at Bykhov Air Base, in the Soviet Republic of Belarus. The radioman on board, Yuriy Kargin, had also previously served at Bykhov Air Base. Their previous connection to the air base came to facilitate their ability to co-operate with the air units from Bykhov that were now deployed.[1]

At 8:30 a.m., nine Tupolev Tu-16K-10-26 medium bombers of the Naval Aviation, took to the air from Bykhov Air Base. At the time, two Naval Aviation regiments with Tu-16K bombers were based at Bykhov: the 240th Guard Bomber Aviation Regiment and the 170th Guard Bomber Aviation Regiment, both of which belonged to the 57th Bomber Aviation Division. The nine Tu-16K bombers were commanded by Colonel Arkhip Dmitriyevich Savinkov, commanding officer of the 240th Guard Bomber Aviation Regiment, and these particular bombers belonged to the regiment's 3rd Squadron. Savinkov's regiment had a long and distinguished history, and its full name was correspondingly lengthy and did not neglect to list the unit's honours: the 240th Guard Sevastopol-Berlin Red Banner Missile Bomber Naval Aviation Regiment (Russian: *240-y gvardeyskiy Sevastopol'sko-Berlinskiy Krasnoznamyonnyy morskoy raketonosnyy aviatsionnyy polk, GvMRAP*). The 240th Regiment belonged to the 57th Bomber Aviation Division, which had a similarly lengthy full name: the 57th Smolensk Red Banner Missile Bomber Naval Aviation Division (Russian: *57-ya Smolenskaya Krasnoznamyonnaya morskaya raketonosnaya aviatsionnaya diviziya, MRAD*).

The Tu-16 was a twin-engine high-speed strategic jet bomber with a crew of seven that had been mass-produced since 1953 and since then had formed the backbone of the Soviet Union's nuclear weapons capacity within Long Range Aviation and Naval Aviation. Originally designed as a high-altitude, free-fall strategic bomber,

An Ilyushin Il-38 maritime partrol and anti-submarine warfare aircraft of the Soviet Naval Aviation. (US DoD)

An overhead view of an Il-38 (Bort 06 Red) in pristine condition, nicely demonstrating its planform and all four engine nacelles – seen at low altitude over the Baltic Sea. (US DoD)

Table 5: Technical characteristics of the Tupolev Tu-16K-10-26 bomber at the time of the 1975 mutiny[2]

General characteristics	
	Length: 34.80 m
	Wingspan: 32.99 m
	Height: 10.36 m
	Wing area: 164.65 m^2
	Empty weight: 37,730 kg
	Gross weight: 72,000 kg
	Maximum takeoff weight: 79,000 kg
	Fuel: 36,000 kg
Thrust	
	2x RD-3M turbojet engines, estimated 93.2 kN thrust each
Performance	
	Maximum speed: 992 km/h
	Cruising speed: 842 km/h
	Range: 7,200 km
	Service ceiling: 15,000 m
	Wing loading: 460 kg/m^2
	Thrust/weight: 0.24
Armament	
	1x Kometa K-10S Luga-S anti-ship missile semi-recessed in bomb bay
	6x 23mm Afanasev Makarov AM-23 cannons, two each in dorsal and ventral remote turrets and manned tail turret
Crew	
	7

the Tu-16 was later developed as a platform for anti-ship missiles. Other variants, based on the same basic airframe and systems, were adapted for respectively reconnaissance, electronic countermeasures (ECM), electronic intelligence (ELINT) collection, and refueling tanker configurations. The Tu-16 had a basically circular section fuselage with a primary pressure cabin at the nose for the crew, with an additional pressure cabin at the tail for the gunner. In-between, the mid-fuselage contained the weapons bay with tankage above, along with a small pressure cabin for the anti-ship missile radar operator. The aircraft's engines occupied the rear part of large ducts added at the wing roots. It was a useful aircraft with good flight characteristics (see Table 5). The Tu-16K bomber entered production in 1958, and Tu-16K-10-26 was a variant used in Naval Aviation since 1970.

Savinkov's aircraft were each armed with one Kometa K-10S Luga-S (ASCC/NATO-codename 'AS-2 Kipper') anti-ship missile. Although we will see that it cannot be conclusively proven, all evidence suggests that during this mission, Savinkov's bomber was armed with a missile with a nuclear warhead. The aircraft's only other armament consisted of two remote turrets and a manned tail turret with a rearward-facing 23mm cannon for self-defence.

The aircraft and its missile constituted a unified weapons system that was exclusively designed to attack US carrier groups. The

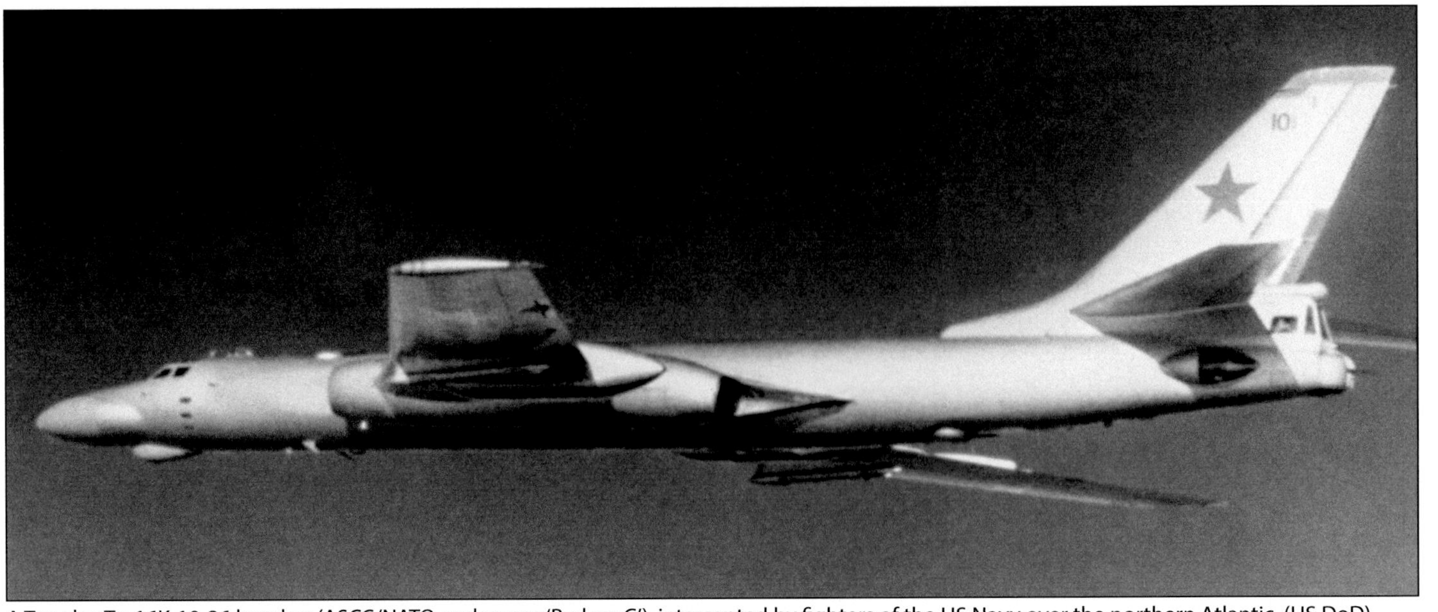

A Tupolev Tu-16K-10-26 bomber (ASCC/NATO-codename 'Badger C'), intercepted by fighters of the US Navy over the northern Atlantic. (US DoD)

A front view of a Tupolev Tu-16K-10-26 bomber (Bort 17 Black), seen being armed with a Kometa K-10S guided air-to-surface missile. (US DoD)

missile existed in two versions, one nuclear-armed and the other conventional.

The Tu-16K bomber was an important weapon in Soviet naval doctrine, which was published from 1960 onwards in a special classified series of documents prepared by the top military command and intended only for army commanders or equivalent and officers above this level.[3] Among other things, the doctrine emphasised that the Soviet Union saw American aircraft carrier groups as a serious threat, because the bombers on board were armed with nuclear weapons and could reach deep into Soviet territory. As a countermeasure, the Soviet Navy therefore intended to use aircraft-borne nuclear-armed anti-ship missiles. And, as the doctrine points out, these had a single purpose – to destroy large ship targets at sea, such as these American aircraft carriers. The task was an exceedingly important one; the Soviets estimated that each American carrier attack force would consist of three carriers, and that each carrier would carry some 140 nuclear bombs, which would be used during the first 72 hours of open warfare. Even if the Soviets managed to destroy 50 percent of the American bombers, they still expected some 200 American nuclear bombs to reach their targets on Soviet soil.[4]

The doctrine accordingly emphasised that aircraft carriers had to be destroyed quickly, before the carrier group reached the point from which its aircraft were within range to carry out missions into Soviet territory. There would be no time for Soviet units to attack enemy naval bases or support vessels. Soviet Naval Aviation must therefore focus on precisely these aircraft carriers during the very first hours of open warfare. Soviet doctrine accordingly emphasised the Tu-16K bombers armed with anti-ship missiles with nuclear warheads as the key weapons system to deploy in the initial phase of combat. While submarines were important, too, they may not arrive in range in time to strike. For this reason, the Tu-16K bombers constituted the first and primary weapon to deploy against the American carrier groups. To succeed, despite the strong protection of the aircraft carrier groups, Soviet doctrine stated that the anti-ship missiles should be fired in salvos. The Soviets did not aim to achieve superiority through a concentration of weapons platforms but through a concentration of missiles. Against an aircraft carrier target, six anti-ship missiles with nuclear warheads would be fired

A close-up view of a Kometa K-10S guided air-to-surface missile (ASCC/NATO-codename 'AS-2 Kipper'), installed semi-recessed under the belly of a Tu-16K-10-26, intercepted by the Swedish Air Force. (Medström)

the target vessel. After all, a nuclear explosion did not have to hit the target directly.

The nine Tu-16K bombers under Colonel Savinkov that took off from Bykhov this morning flew in groups of three, according to current doctrine. From about 9:10 a.m., the groups gradually arrived in the area where the *Storozhevoy* had been found. The first group of three was led by Colonel Savinkov himself, with aircraft from the 3rd Squadron under Bakholdin. The second group of three came from the 2nd Squadron and was led by its commander, Tikhiy. Shortly after the aircraft took off from Bykhov Air Base, the

at the same time, three from one direction and three from another.[5] This was because during the testing of the K-10 system (tests began in 1958 but the system was only taken into service in 1961), it had been found that the missile's accuracy rate was only 80 percent.[6] The guidance procedure was by necessity complex. In order for the missile to carry out the final dive towards its target ship, the radar had to be locked on target. To that end, a Tu-16K bomber after launch flew in a run around the target while keeping its radar locked on it. The missile had to be launched at least 110km from the target, or the onboard guidance mechanism would not have time to aim it correctly.[7] Yet, even so every fifth anti-ship missile launched navigated incorrectly. Under these circumstances, it was obvious that a nuclear warhead was necessary to ensure the destruction of

Storozhevoy passed through the Irben Sound in the regular sea lane. She then turned north, first to a course of 340 degrees, then 325 degrees. So far, she stayed in the regular sea lane.

It was now that the utility of the fact that the crews of the Anti-Submarine Warfare Aviation Squadron in Riga were familiar with the airmen from Bykhov became clear. Captain Grishkin's Il-38 from Riga henceforth followed and reported the *Storozhevoy*'s movements to Colonel Savinkov's bombers. The Naval Aviation pilots thus had a good idea of what was happening down at sea level. This was necessary, because the visibility was poor and the cloud base was only 600 to 700 metres above sea level.[8] Above the clouds there was no opportunity to see what was happening below. Grishkin's radioman, Kargin, also transited radio communications between Riga and the bombers, which at times was required to secure communications.

The crew of a Tu-16K-10-26 in front of their bomber, planning a mission. Notable is the large bulge of the powerful search radar, used to guide the K-10S missile. (Medström)

Colonel Savinkov, who flew first, reached the *Storozhevoy* with the first group of three Tu-16K bombers. The other two groups of three arrived a little later. He went down at low altitude, under the clouds, to read the bow number of the ship. The mission at that stage was to try to make the mutineers realise the inevitable and surrender. For obvious reasons, an anti-ship missile was not the optimal weapon system to persuade a mutineer to surrender. Since each aircraft only carried one missile, there was no way to fire a warning shot, and a live missile discharge was likely to sink a warship the size of the *Storozhevoy*. As a result, Colonel Savinkov and his men descended until they could fire warning shots with the rearward-facing cannon.

An overhead view of a Tu-16K-10-26 underway above a broken cloud, relatively low over the Baltic Sea. (US DoD)

For one hour from about 9:15 a.m. onwards, Savinkov's bombers made repeated approaches at altitudes of from 100 to 500 metres towards the *Storozhevoy*. Nothing else was possible either; the cloud base meant that the only chance to identify the ship was to go down at low altitude and read its bow number. The airmen had visual contact with the *Storozhevoy* and fired repeated warning shots with automatic cannon. However, the cannon fire failed to compel the *Storozhevoy* to surrender. Savinkov then sought to gain a psychological advantage over the mutineers by increasing the power of the jet engines just as the 35-metre-long bombers passed right next to the ship at low altitude, something that should have been perceived as more physically frightening than the actual warning shots. The *Storozhevoy* was only four times longer than a Tu-16K bomber – and she was a large warship. Through these manoeuvres, the airmen repeatedly forced the *Storozhevoy* to deviate from the main course, which was 325 degrees, as she took evasive action to avoid the bypasses and overflights. After repeated such approaches, *Storozhevoy* turned west at about 10:05 a.m., at a course of 250 degrees, perhaps in an attempt to go straight towards the Swedish island of Gotland. Although Sablin said that he did not harbour any such intention, and later explained that he never aimed to move into Swedish waters, we cannot say with certainty how the repeated bypasses and overflights affected him and the bridge crew.

Sablin later stuck to the story that he was only taking evasive action. Yet, the *Storozhevoy*'s evasive manoeuvres made it even more difficult for the Soviet commanders to assess where she was actually heading. It should be remembered that her final destination had been unclear to the Soviets ever since the pursuit began. They had only Sablin's word to Firsov as evidence that he really intended to sail for Leningrad. Sablin's telegrams had been deliberately vague on the *Storozhevoy*'s destination. Moreover, the normal course for a ship bound for Leningrad, after passing through the Irben Sound, was 337 degrees.[9] But the *Storozhevoy*'s apparent main course, 325 degrees, went in a slightly more westerly direction, which would have taken the ship to the Stockholm Archipelago in Sweden. The course suggested that the *Storozhevoy* was heading for Swedish waters. Perhaps one can suspect that Sablin was not on his way to Leningrad after all, despite what he claimed in his speech to the crew. It would certainly have been a more prudent move for a determined revolutionary to seek safety in Swedish waters, from which he could make his appeal to the United Nations, than to sail straight into a Soviet naval base. Moreover, during the heat of the action, the Soviets could easily interpret the *Storozhevoy*'s movements as her aiming directly for Sweden. On the appropriate course, it would take the *Storozhevoy* only two and a half hours to reach safety in Swedish waters.

5
FRONTAL AVIATION STRIKES

The Minister of Defence, Marshal of the Soviet Union Andrey Grechko, had already anticipated that warning shots would not be enough to make the mutineers give up.

Therefore, he had sent another air unit into the air: the 668th Bomber Aviation Regiment (Russian: *668-y bombardirovochnyy aviatsionnyy polk, BAP*), which belonged to the 15th Tactical Air Army of Frontal Aviation in the Baltic military district. The regiment had its home in Tukums Air Base just outside the well-known Soviet beach resort of Jurmala (present Jūrmala) in Latvia. The regiment was equipped with Yakovlev Yak-28 (ASCC/NATO-codename 'Brewer') tactical bombers (see Table 6). The Yak-28 was an older twin-engine aircraft with a crew of two, whose main task in war was to attack enemy air bases. The type first flew in 1958 and entered service in 1960.

The crews the 668th Bomber Aviation Regiment were not part of Naval Aviation, had no experience of operations against naval targets, and had limited knowledge of warships.

The alarm reportedly went off at the air base at approximately 3:00 a.m., that is, approximately at the same time as within the Baltic Fleet. The headquarters of the 15th Tactical Air Army, to which the regiment belonged, then announced that a foreign warship – some form of missile destroyer with two anti-aircraft missile launchers –

Soviet naval uniforms as of 1973. Left to right: parade uniform No. 1, for summer use; parade uniform No. 2, for summer use; parade uniform No. 3 for officers, for summer use; parade uniform No. 4 for officers, for winter use. (Soviet Ministry of Defence)

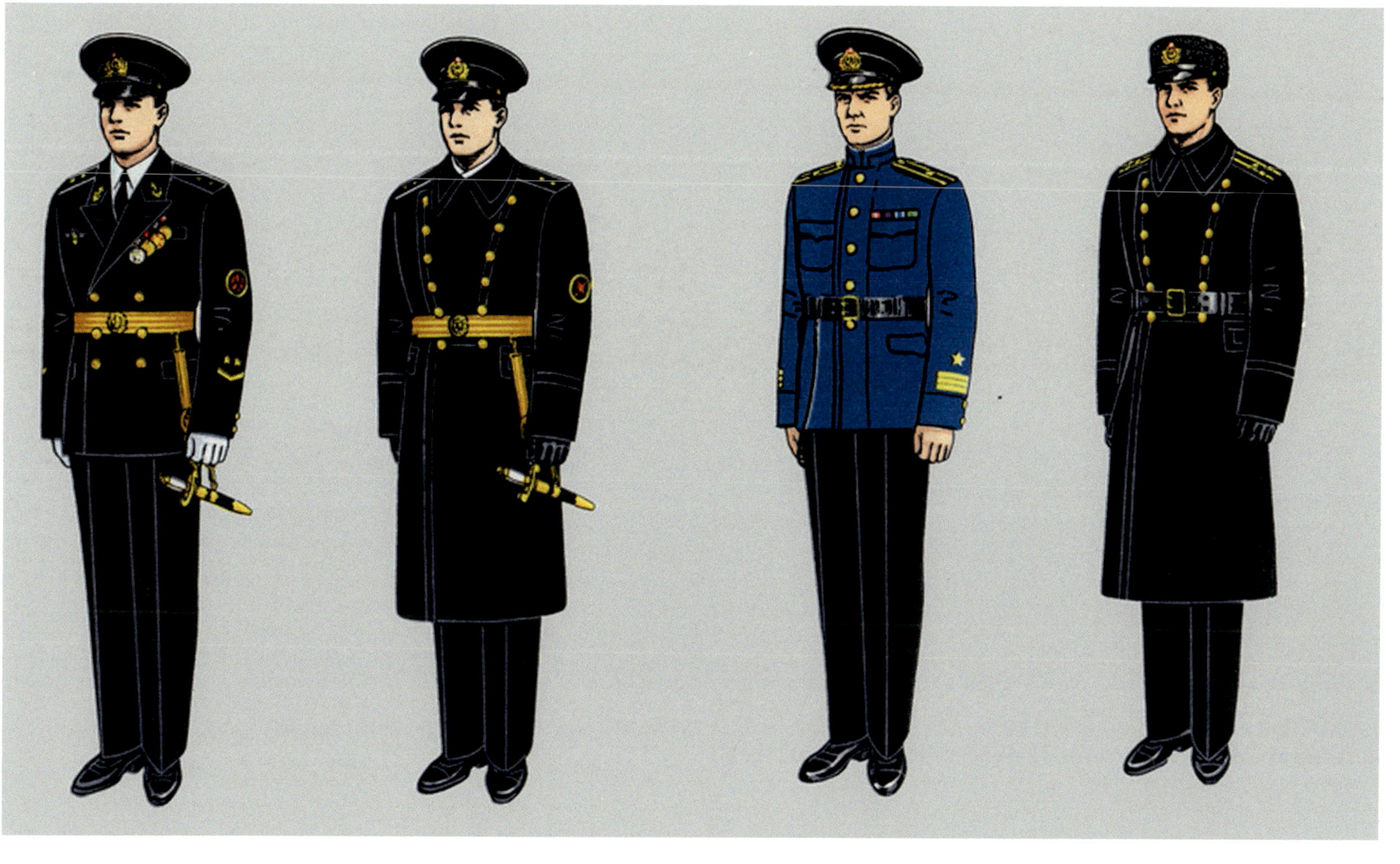

Soviet naval uniforms, 1973. Left to right: Parade uniform No. 3 for warrant officers, for summer use; parade uniform No. 4 for warrant officers, for winter use; daily duty uniform No. 3, for summer use; daily duty uniform No. 4 (with cap, illustrated here) and No. 5 (with fur cap), for winter use. (Soviet Ministry of Defence)

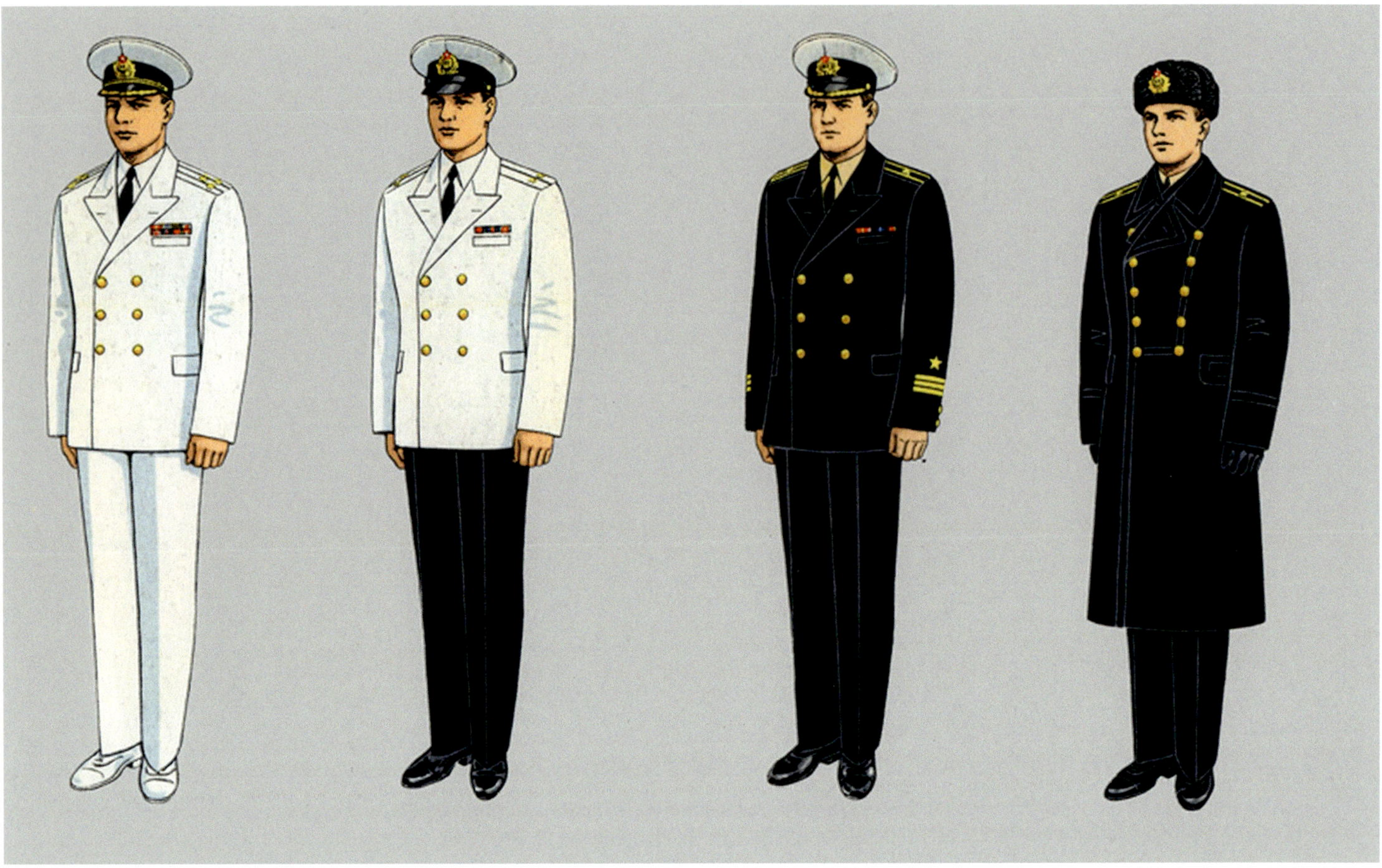

Soviet naval uniforms, 1973. Left to right: daily off-duty uniform No. 1, for summer use; daily off-duty uniform No. 2, for summer use; daily off-duty uniform No. 3, for summer use; daily off-duty uniform No. 4 (with cap) and No. 5 (with fur cap, as illustrated here), for winter use. (Soviet Ministry of Defence)

An anti-submarine warfare vessel of the Project 1135 Burevestnik-class (ASCC/NATO-codename 'Krivak I') seen in the early 1980s. Note all side-surfaces painted in mid-grey and the deck painted in rust-red. (US DoD)

Kapitan of the Baltic Fleet, shown in the formal officers' uniform, including a black winter overcoat with the insignia of the Baltic Fleet on the left shoulder, and the typical Ushanka cap, in this case with the navy headdress. (Artwork by Anderson Subtil)

A crewman of a Tupolev Tu-16 bomber of the Soviet Naval Aviation, shown wearing the ShL-58 leather flight helmet (which, although nominally obsolete, offered much greater comfort during long missions than any of the subsequent rigid models), the Sz-50 flight suit (composed of a heavy jacket and padded pants with suspenders), and leather-lined flight boots with side-zipper. (Artwork by Anderson Subtil)

A typical Yak-28 pilot of the mid-1970s, shown wearing the ZSh-3M flight helmet, and Sz-54 summer flight suit, with a light jacket atop it – as widely used not only by the Soviet Air Force, but also many customers abroad. (Artwork by Anderson Subtil)

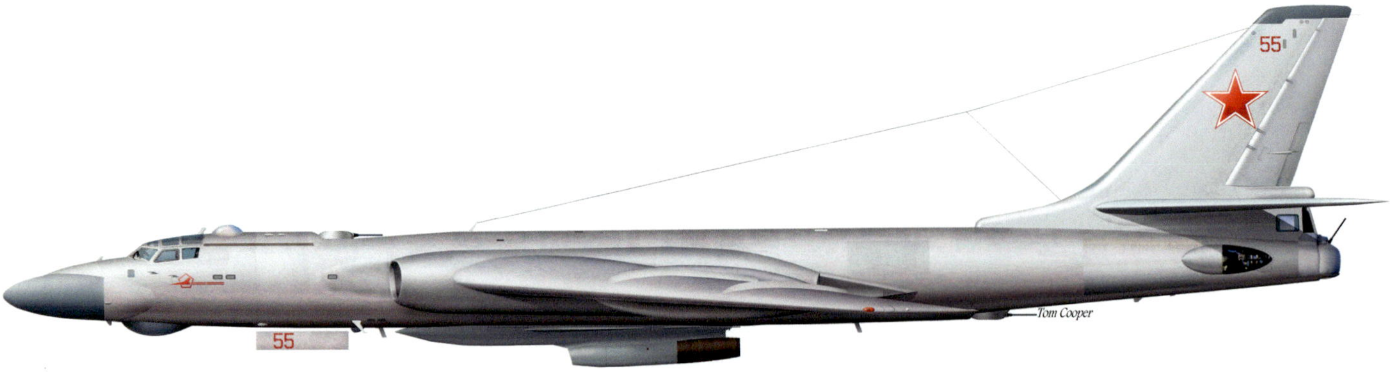

The Tupolev Tu-16K-10-16 was a variant of this medium bomber family developed specifically for the Naval Aviation, and capable of carrying a single K-10S anti-ship missile (ASCC/NATO-codename 'AS-2 Kipper'). For its mission, it had a large search radar in an extended radome on the nose, while the K-10S was installed semi-recessed under the centre fuselage. Exactly 216 Tu-16K-10s were manufactured between 1958 and 1963. The precise appearance of the two Tu-16K-10-16s of the 240th Guards Bomber Air Regiment involved in the pursuit of *Storozhevoy* remains unknown, but as of the mid-1970s, all of these wore the same overall livery in two layers of clear lacquer, mixed with 10 percent and 5 percent aluminium powder, respectively. The only markings consisted of national insignia, the well-known 'Bort number' (55 in red, applied near the top of the fin and on the cover of the front undercarriage bay), and the crest of 'excellence' applied below the cockpit. (Artwork by Tom Cooper)

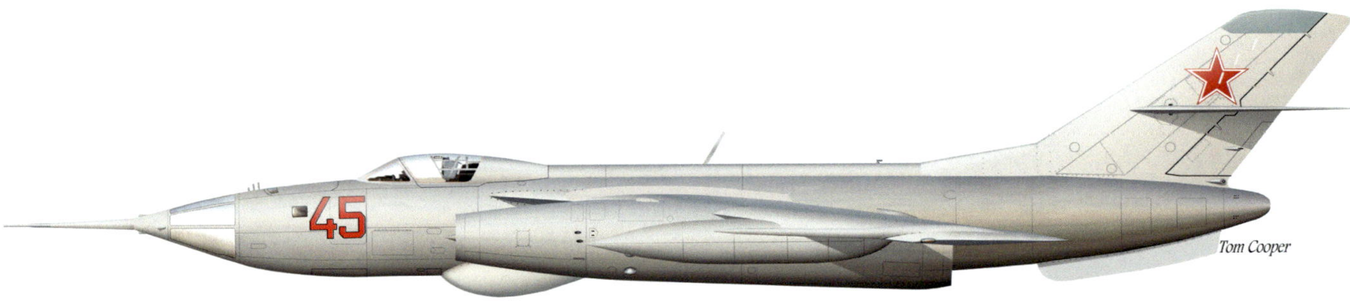

The Yakovlev Yak-28 was a swept-wing fighter-bomber powered by two turbojets installed in gondolas underneath the wing. A total of 1,180 were manufactured between during the first half of the 1960s, of which 223 were the Yak-28I, dedicated tactical bomber, illustrated here. The jet was subsonic (it could breach the sound barrier only when underway at high altitude), and had an internal bomb bay, including the capability for deployment of tactical nuclear weapons. While its pilot was seated inside a classic cockpit, the navigator was positioned in front of him in the transparent forward fuselage, and (in the variant Yak-28L, one of which participated in the mission) in front of a radome for the RSBN-2 radar, installed underneath the fuselage to provide a 360-degree coverage. In addition to tactical nuclear weapons, the Yak-28I could be armed with bombs of up to 500kg, or UB-16-57 pods for 57mm S-5K unguided rockets. Sadly, the exact appearance of the two examples from 668th BAP involved in the pursuit of the *Storozhevoy* remains unknown, but 'Red 45' illustrated here is representative of their livery in the early 1970s: this consisted of two layers of clear lacquer, mixed with 10 percent and 5 percent aluminium powder, respectively. (Artwork by Tom Cooper)

The Ilyushin Il-38 was a maritime patrol and anti-submarine warfare aircraft developed from the Ilyushin Il-18 transport and powered by four turboprop engines. Only some 58 were ever manufactured during the first half of the 1960s, but they saw intensive service with Soviet Naval Aviation units assigned to the Northern, Pacific, and Baltic Fleets. The precise appearance of the Il-38s of the 145th Independent Anti-Submarine Warfare Aviation Squadron remains unknown: the example here is shown wearing the standard livery in mid-grey, national markings (applied in six positions, as on all Soviet military aircraft), and the 'Bort' 15 in red, high on the fin. (Artwork by Tom Cooper)

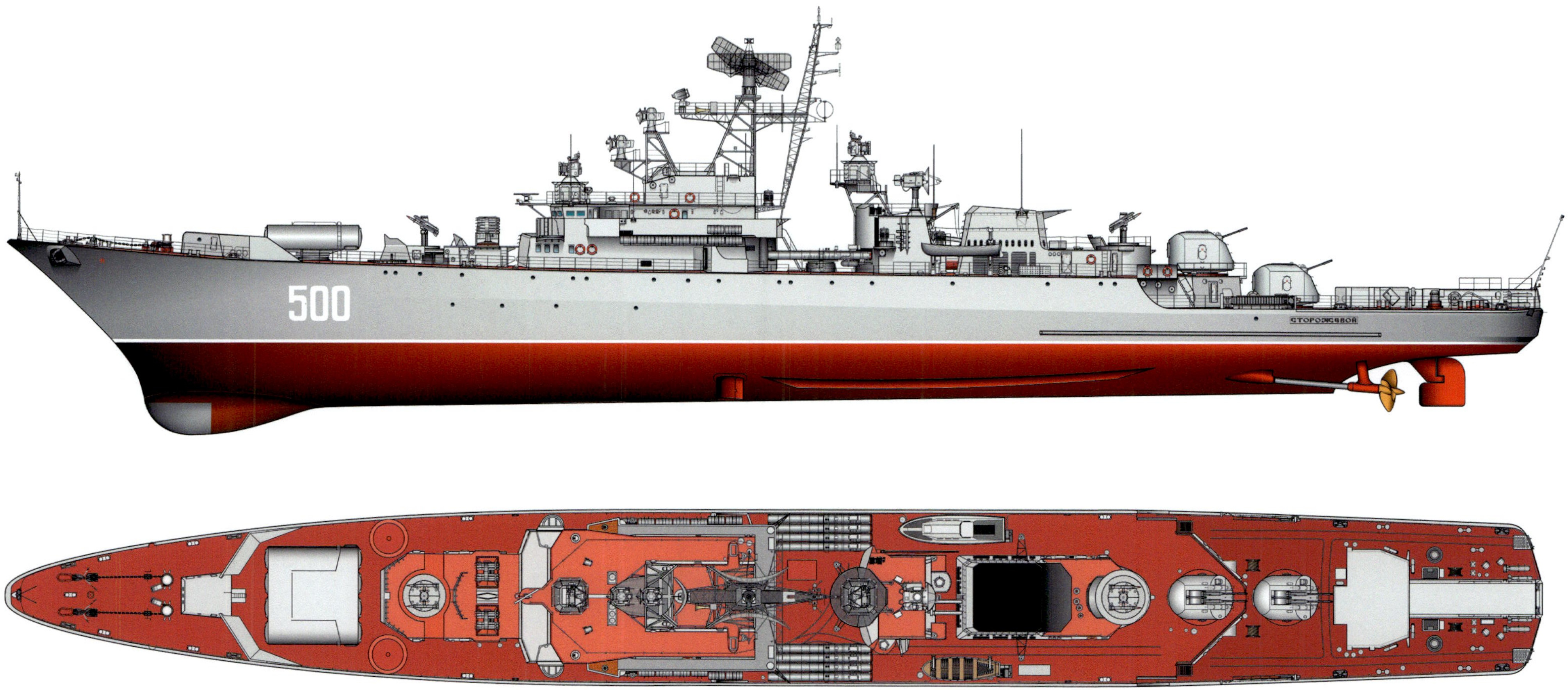

The *Storozhevoy* (Russian for 'guardian' or 'sentry') was an anti-submarine vessel of the Project 1135 Burevestnik-class (NATO-codename 'Krivak I'), attached to the Soviet Baltic Fleet and based in Baltiysk. Constructed by Yantar Shipbuilding in Kaliningrad between July 1972 and December 1973 and commissioned into service with the Baltic Fleet on 30 December 1973, she was powered by gas turbines. Primary mission equipment comprised an anti-submarine warfare combat system consisting of a single URPK-4 Metel' launcher for four 85R anti-ship missiles (ASCC/NATO-codename 'SS-N-14 Silex'), two RBU-6000 multiple launchers for anti-submarine rocket depth charges, and two launchers for four 533mm torpedoes. Air defence was provided by two Osa-M launchers (ASCC/NATO-codename 'SA-N-4 Gecko'). Finally, each of two turrets atop the aft section of the hull were equipped with AK-726 twin-barrel 76mm guns. (Artwork by Ivan Zajac)

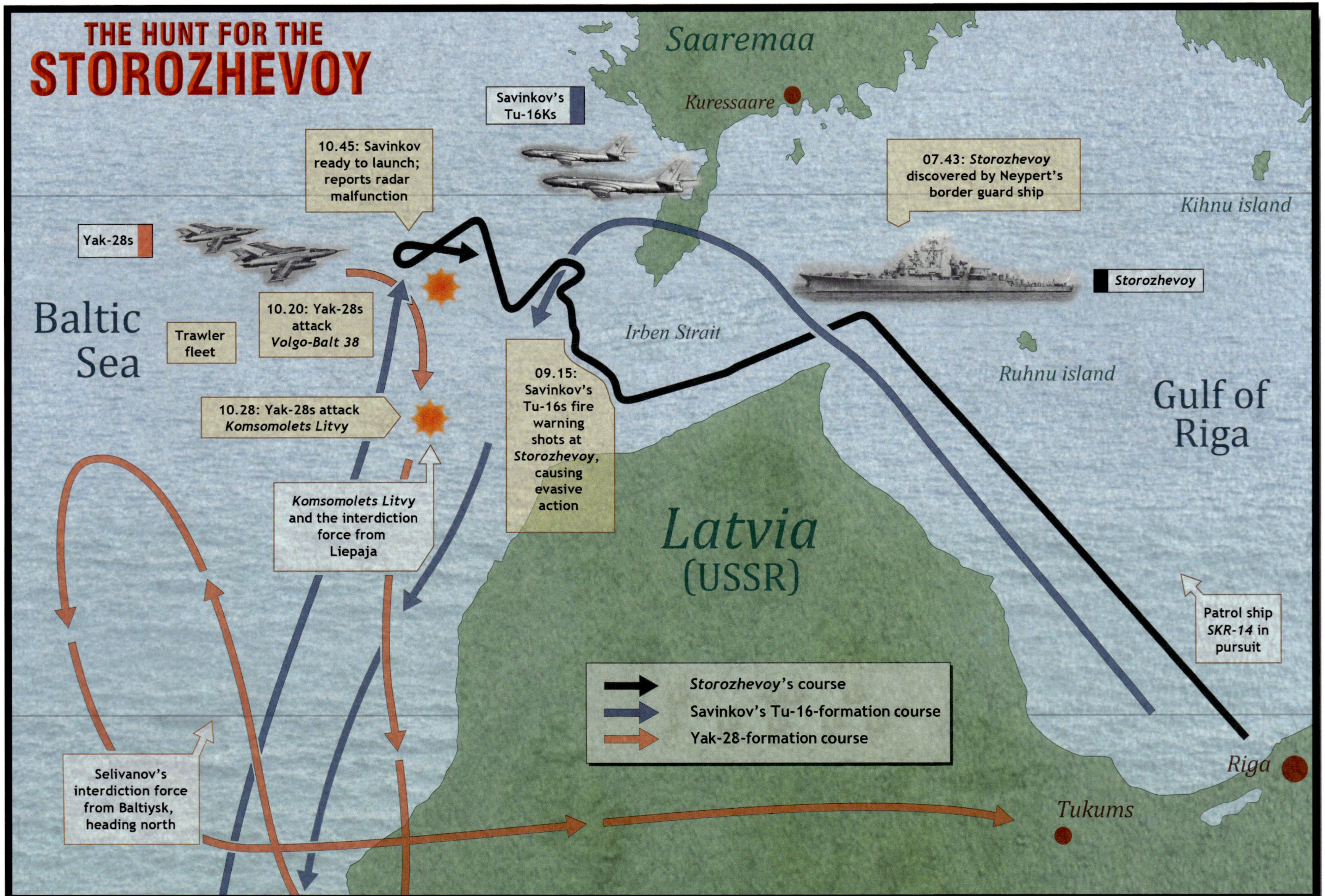

The *Storozhevoy*'s movement during the mutiny on 9 November 1975. No Soviet unit detected the *Storozhevoy* before she passed through the Irben Sound between the Bay of Riga and the Baltic Sea. However, the Swedish SIGINT service monitored her in real time ever since she left the River Daugava and set out into the Bay of Riga. The SIGINT service also monitored the *Storozhevoy*'s evasive action as Sablin attempted to outmanoeuvre the Tu-16K bombers and the guard ships of the KGB Border Troops. Her evasive action could easily be interpreted as attempts to reach Swedish territorial waters. There was certainly nothing in the *Storozhevoy*'s movements that suggested that Sablin intended to sail to Leningrad. To the Soviets, the suspicion that Sablin intended to defect to Sweden seemed confirmed by the *Storozhevoy*'s movements. The map is entirely based on the Swedish SIGINT service's carefully plotted record of the *Storozhevoy*'s movements. (Map by Anderson Subtil)

A a Yak-28L fighter-bomber seen while landing. Notable are the radome for the RSBN-2 radar installed under the fuselage, the planform with two engine nacelles, auxiliary fuel tanks installed under outboard wing portions, and the unusual configuration of its landing gear. (US DoD)

Table 6: Technical characteristics of the Yakovlev Yak-28 tactical bomber at the time of the 1975 mutiny[3]

General characteristics	
	Length: 20.02 m
	Wingspan: 11.78 m
	Height: 4.3 m
	Wing area: 35.25 m^2
	Empty weight: 9,970 kg
	Gross weight: 16,160 kg
	Maximum takeoff weight: 18,080 kg
	Fuel: Depending on configuration
Thrust	
	2x R-11AF-300 afterburning turbojet engines, 46 kN thrust each dry, 59.8 kN with afterburner
Performance	
	Maximum speed: 1,850 km/h
	Cruising speed: 1,040 km/h
	Range: 2,070 km
	Service ceiling: 14,500 m
	Wing loading: 531 kg/m^2
	Thrust/weight: 0.62
Armament	
	4x 250-kg free-fall fragmentation bombs type OFAB-250Sh (under normal circumstances a bomb load of up to 1,200 kg)
	1x 23mm NR-23 or GSh-23 forward-aiming fixed gun (50 rounds)
Crew	
	2

had penetrated the Gulf of Riga. The regiment was ordered to be ready to attack and sink the foreign ship.[1] The description of the ship's general size and armament was thus correct, even though at this stage nobody dared to give the airmen her true identity. The foreign ship was probably described as West German, because that at least was what the rumour that soon spread within the Soviet Baltic Fleet indicated.[2]

In the morning, Tukums Air Base was reportedly informed by telephone about the location of the warship – in the Irben Sound. Taking off before first light, the commander of the 2nd Squadron of the 668th Bomber Aviation Regiment for about three quarters of an hour from approximately 8:00 a.m. carried out a reconnaissance mission within the planned area of operations. It was important to investigate the weather conditions there – they were as usual in the morning of an autumn day over the Baltic Sea, that is, quite poor – but he also had the task of trying to find the enemy ship. Within the regiment there were two versions of the Yak-28. The majority were Yak-28Is that were only equipped with radar sights for bombing. However, the squadron commander flew a Yak-28L, which had a navigation radar of the RSBN-2 type and therefore could have determined the *Storozhevoy*'s exact position if she had been spotted. However, the squadron commander failed to locate her.[4] There is no indication that the airmen in Tukums knew that Captain Grishkin in his Il-38 had already located

A cargo ship of the Volgo-Balt type. It may seem surprising that the crews of the 668th Bomber Aviation Regiment mistook a transport of this kind for the *Storozhevoy*. However, the regiment belonged to the Frontal Aviation, not Naval Aviation, and had never practised operations against maritime targets. It is extremely unlikely that any of them had ever seen even a photograph of the ship they were looking for: unsurprisingly, they had no idea what *Storozhevoy* looked like – and especially not when seeing the ship from above while the visibility was hampered by the cloud cover. (Medström)

the *Storozhevoy* and that Colonel Savinkov's Tu-16K bomber at the same moment as the Yak-28 was out at sea was actually rolling out on the runway. The two organisations, Naval Aviation and Frontal Aviation, had no established contacts other than significantly higher up in the hierarchy.

According to some information, it was the Minister of Defence, Grechko, who personally ordered the regiment in Tukums to attack the *Storozhevoy* and sink her, if necessary.[5] This would also be in accordance with the logical chain of command, as the 15th Tactical Air Army was not part of Naval Aviation and thus was not under Admiral Gorshkov's command.

One may wonder why Grechko, a Marshal of the Soviet Union and with long experience of the Soviet Armed Forces, would give the assignment to a regiment that did not even belong to Naval Aviation, which already had Tu-16K bombers ready to take off. Grechko may have suspected that the naval pilots would not want to attack comrades from their own fleet. If so, he worried needlessly; as we shall see, there is little or nothing to suggest that the naval pilots refused to carry out their mission. More likely, Grechko realised that the Tu-16K bombers had the wrong kind of weapons load for the mission. Automatic cannon fire hardly impressed the fugitive ship (and was intended to be used only for self-defence, not offensive attacks), and the Tu-16K bomber pilots' remaining weapons, anti-ship missiles, were lethal weapons whose use could only have one outcome. For the Tu-16K bomber crews, the options for weapon deployment were comparable to the choice between a pen knife and a sledgehammer. The weapons load was carefully selected for the aircraft's regular task and not dimensioned for anything else.

For the Yak-28 pilots, the mission had come as a complete surprise. Not only was it Sunday and the morning after the Day of the Great October Socialist Revolution, traditionally celebrated with heavy drinking, the mission was also to be carried out over the sea and against targets of a type against which they had never practised. The bomber aviation regiment belonged to Frontal Aviation, which was intended to support the Ground Forces, not the Navy. Everything about the mission was completely new to the regiment, and none of it had ever been practised. Immediate planning began for the new mission, but there was uncertainty about most things, and in the midst of it all, the Commander of 15th Tactical Air Army, Major General Boris Gvozdikov, suddenly called personally to give detailed tactical instructions on how to carry out the attack. Gvozdikov, an old Second World War air force hero and reconnaissance veteran, himself admitted that the situation was unclear. But the mission was urgent, and everything must be done in a hurry. Following wartime protocol, Gvozdikov ordered the entire regiment to take off immediately, so that there would be no aircraft left on the ground if something went wrong.[6]

As a result, the aircraft took off as soon as possible, with the weapons load already at hand: 250-kg free-fall fragmentation bombs. There was therefore some confusion at the airport when the first Yak-28s were to roll out for takeoff. They only received a description of their target when the first planes were in the air.

At 10:00 a.m., there were about 20 Yak-28s in the air. At about 10:20 a.m., the Yak-28s carried out attacks with bombs from a height of between 400 and 500 metres towards what they thought was the *Storozhevoy*. The attack was led by Lieutenant Colonel A. Porotikov, who was very experienced and had been with the 668th Bomber Aviation Regiment ever since it was based in Tukum in 1968.[7]

The problem was, however, that it was not the *Storozhevoy* which they bombed. It was soon obvious to the airmen that they had attacked the wrong target, because when the Yak-28s dropped a series of bombs next to the ship, its crew immediately radioed for help. Fortunately, this made everyone involved understand that it was the wrong target.[8] The attack could be aborted before anybody was killed or wounded. The target was not a warship at all, but the Soviet cargo ship *Volgo-Balt 38*, en route from the Latvian port Ventspils to Finland. With a length of 114m and beam of 13m, she was roughly the same size as the *Storozhevoy*, which had a length

A nice study of a Yak-28 prototype in flight: notably, this still lacked the radome under the fuselage, and had a slightly different configuration of transparencies in the forward fuselage compared to the Yak-28I fighter-bomber. The jet's primary weapon – either a nuclear bomb, or conventional bomb of up to 1,500kg – was always intended to be carried internally. (Amphalon)

of 123m and a beam of 14.2m. While *Volgo-Balt 38* differed in appearance, when seen directly from above the differences were less obvious. Besides, visibility was poor because of the low cloud base.

Lieutenant Colonel Porotikov and his men then continued the search for the mutineer elsewhere. The airmen from Tukums Air Base now believed that the target must be near the Swedish island of Gotland. Finally, they discovered what looked like a group of warships. However, since they had attacked the wrong target already once, this time the pilots took greater care and went down to an altitude of 200 metres to identify the target visually. Which was lucky, as the vessels turned out to be a fleet of trawlers.[9]

In the end, despite the difficulties the airmen found the right naval force: the *Storozhevoy* and the Soviet warships of the pursuit force. The cloud base was still at an altitude of 600 to 700 metres, so it was difficult visually to get an overview of the situation. After the mistake with the cargo ship, the pilots received repeated orders to attack only when the *Storozhevoy* had been positively identified, and now they finally got their target, a proper warship of the right appearance, in their sights. There may originally have been a perception that bombs should only be dropped for warning purposes, but this time, at 10:28 a.m., the pilots were ordered to attack 'straight at him'.[10]

Now the *Storozhevoy* would be hit, not just warned. Four minutes later, a Yak-28 dropped bombs which fell 50 metres in front of – not the *Storozhevoy*, but the slightly smaller *Komsomolets Litvy*, the lead warship of the pursuit force from which Captain First Rank Rassukovannyy commanded the chase of the *Storozhevoy*! Being inexperienced in naval matters, the Frontal Aviation airmen had failed to spot the difference between the two warships.

The bomb fragments spread far and wide, and a fire broke out on the *Komsomolets Litvy*.[11] Rassukovannyy's ships were then 16.5km behind the *Storozhevoy*, but the Yak-28 pilots, unfamiliar with naval targets as they were and without clear information about the target, had simply not been able to tell the difference between the warships. The *Komsomolets Litvy* fired signal rockets to make the Yak-28 pilots understand that they were attacking the wrong target, but there was doubt among the pilots as to whether these were signal rockets or muzzle flashes from anti-aircraft artillery. Only when the Yak-28 pilots finally realised that the flames were signal rockets did they also realise that they had attacked the wrong ship. But then someone on the warship opened fire at them with a machine gun. Fortunately, the machine gun fire did not hit.[12]

6
NUCLEAR LAUNCH PROTOCOL

About the same time as the Tukums bombers had taken off and were about to begin their mission, Grechko and Gorshkov from their headquarters in Moscow ordered the commander of Naval Aviation of the Baltic Fleet, Sergey Gulyayev, Colonel General of the Air Force, Hero of the Soviet Union, and Second World War veteran, to commence preparations for sinking the *Storozhevoy*.[1]

Gulyayev took the task seriously. At 10:00 a.m., the ships of the pursuit force were ordered to move away from the *Storozhevoy* and seek a safe distance, as a group of Tu-16K bombers were on their way. It was Colonel Savinkov's small force of Tu-16K bombers which now made a new approach towards the *Storozhevoy*. All ships were instructed to position themselves at least 10km behind the *Storozhevoy*. 'Now the air force will act', a message from the Main Directorate of Border Troops informed Neypert's force.[2]

This time the sledgehammer, not the pen knife, would be used. As noted, each Tu-16K bomber carried only one anti-ship missile, the nearly ten-metre-long Kometa K-10S Luga-S. We have seen that in order for the missile to carry out the final dive towards the target vessel, the radar was required to be locked on target. To that end, a Tu-16K bomber after launch would keep its radar locked on the

This rare photograph is one of very few authentic documents about operations to find and destroy *Storozhevoy*. Taken by a pilot of a Saab 37 Viggen interceptor of the Swedish Air Force, it shows three Tu-16K bombers in the standard combat formation during their attack run over the Baltic Sea. (Medström)

A Tupolev Tu-16 cockpit from the inside. While not always flying the same individual aircraft, Soviet bomber crews were kept together and had the time to get to know and trust each other. During the Cold War, a typical crew would spend many hours in flight, in particular those who were on combat alert duty in case of a surprise attack on the Motherland. The Tu-16K crews belonged to this category. (Medström)

target. In addition, the missile must be launched at least 110km from the target, or the onboard steering mechanism would not have time to aim it correctly.

Colonel General Gulyayev had ordered Colonel Savinkov only to launch an anti-ship missile on his direct order.[3] Gulyayev may have decided to lead the attack from the front. During the morning, a dedicated command and control aircraft had taken off from Khrabrovo Air Base outside Kaliningrad, where the Baltic Fleet's headquarters was located, and Gulyayev's orders were either transited via or sent directly from this aircraft. It is quite possible that Gulyayev himself was onboard. By all accounts, he was a man who would lead from the front, and this time, the situation was critical. At 10:16 a.m., Gulyayev personally ordered Colonel Savinkov and his unit to prepare for weapons launch against the *Storozhevoy* from an altitude of 4,000 metres at a range of, as far as can be ascertained, 160 km. Immediately afterwards, still at 10:16 a.m., Gulyayev gave the order 'use the weapon'. In addition, he executed the special protocol for the launch of nuclear missiles. This protocol necessitated a mutual confirmation of the launch order so as to avoid any chance of error. On his side, Gulyayev confirmed the launch order at 10:27 a.m., in a communication in part transited by radioman Kargin on Captain Grishkin's Il-38.

Savinkov now only had to place his aircraft in position and at the right distance to launch his missile.

At this very moment, in the command post of the headquarters of the Baltic Fleet, Vice Admiral Kosov sat with one telephone receiver in each hand. In one, he received instructions from Defence Minister Grechko (who presumably already had forgotten that he earlier in the morning had delegated the task to handle the situation to Admiral Gorshkov). In the other telephone receiver, Kosov forwarded Grechko's orders to Colonel General Gulyayev. The Tu-16K bombers were on course for the target, and the three men were well aware that the nuclear launch protocol had been confirmed. Then, suddenly, the head of the Operations Directorate, Rear Admiral Yakovlev, ran into the room. According to an eyewitness, Yakovlev shouted: 'The *Storozhevoy* has halted, Comrade Commander. We must abort the attack on her!'[4] We do not know what Kosov reported to Grechko or what he said to Gulyayev, but certainly men at the command post at this point began to issue orders, down along the various chains of command, to abort the attack.

Meanwhile, Rassukovannyy's pursuit force was not far from the *Storozhevoy*. Probably at 10:37 a.m., its commander either received countermanding orders from higher up in the chain of command, or he realised that something was amiss. At 10:44 a.m., the moment before Savinkov was to launch his anti-ship missile, frantic radio messages from the *Komsomolets Litvy* and her sister ship, the aforementioned SKR-14 which had set out from Riga 45 minutes after the *Storozhevoy*, ordered 'everyone in the air' to 'suspend the use of weapons'.

But either Savinkov did not hear the order, because of the use of different radio channels, or he interpreted it as not intended for him but for the Yak-28 pilots, to make them leave the area. After all, he had received his order to launch directly from Colonel General Gulyayev. Still, Savinkov did not launch his anti-ship missile. At 10:45 a.m., he explained to the others in the group of three that his radar had malfunctioned. The magnetron had failed, Savinkov reported. Without an operational magnetron, a high-power vacuum tube then used in radar systems and notorious for the time it took to start up, Savinkov's missile was blind. Otherwise, Savinkov appeared to be in position, but since the anti-ship missile had to be guided by radar, he could not launch. Savinkov therefore ordered the other two bombers to attack the *Storozhevoy* independently.

For another 60 seconds, the remaining two Tu-16K bombers prepared to launch their anti-ship missiles. At the same time, various Soviet radiomen frantically tried to convey the order to suspend the attack to the Tu-16K bombers. Finally, the order for 'everyone in the air' finally went through. At 10:46, Savinkov ordered his men to abort the attack. No missile was launched.

7
THE SURRENDER

What Savinkov could not know was that on the *Storozhevoy*, the overflights, cannon fire, and bombings had given the crew cold feet.

Even the first Tu-16K bomber overflights had been frightening to the mutineers, who perhaps only then began to realise that the Motherland now regarded them as traitors. The ensuing automatic cannon fire and then the bombing shattered the courage and will of the already demoralised mutineers to continue. Some sailors realised where it was headed and at 10:20 a.m., a group of them under Seaman Lykov freed Captain Potul'nyy and the other detained officers.[1] These armed themselves and then stormed the warship's command bridge. During the commotion, Sablin was shot in the leg and disarmed. The crew locked him up. Captain Potul'nyy immediately sent a message that the mutiny was over, he had restored control of the situation, and awaited orders. Then they signalled to the pursuit force that they surrendered. It was at 10:32 a.m., exactly five minutes after Savinkov's order to launch missile had been confirmed by the commander of Naval Aviation of the Baltic Fleet.[2] The mutiny was over.

At 11:00 a.m., the now somewhat fire-ravaged *Komsomolets Litvy* with Captain First Rank Rassukovannyy on board reached the *Storozhevoy*, the officers of which contacted the pursuing ships by radio and announced that their vessel was ready to be boarded.

The pursuers then approached the *Storozhevoy* but with some caution, apparently prepared for the worst. The *Komsomolets Litvy* and her sister ship, the aforementioned SKR-14, cast anchor a few hundred metres away, probably to cover the boarding force. One of the Il-38s from Riga stayed nearby to monitor the situation from the air, and its crew reported to the pursuit force what was happening on the *Storozhevoy*. The boarding force moored at about 11:15 a.m. next to the *Storozhevoy*. Onboard the *Storozhevoy*, the crew began

A group photo of the *Storozhevoy*'s crew from 1974. Sablin and Potul'nyy are visible in the front row, centre, with their caps in their hands.. (Author's Collection)

An Il-38 maritime patrol aircraft passing low over a Burevestnik/Krivak-I during an exercise in 1979. (US DoD)

A Tarantul-class border patrol vessel and a Tu-16 bomber, seen escorting *Storozhevoy* during the mutiny. (Author's Collection)

to go up on deck, where they waited for the boarding force. The first boarding force was not large, only 15 sailors personally led by Captain First Rank Rassukovannyy. He himself arrived unarmed, but his men carried weapons.[3]

Another 10 Tu-16K bombers from Bykhov Air Base had now reached the area of operation. They were not needed for the operation itself, so they instead began patrolling the sea from high altitude, flying two runs between the island of Saaremaa and Liepaja Naval Base. They remained in the area for a couple of hours.

At 11:40 a.m., the *Storozhevoy*, surrounded by four or five border guard ships, began to move at a course of 90 degrees, back to the Soviet coastline. Half an hour later, Vice Admiral Kosov, the commanding officer of the Baltic Fleet, announced to his subordinate naval bases and to Valentin Selivanov, en route with his pursuit force from Baltiysk, that the crisis was over.

During the morning, warships from the 12th Missile Ship Squadron in Baltiysk had also been ordered to take part in the operation. This was the unit to which the *Storozhevoy* belonged. Since about 10:00 a.m., three warships were heading north under the command of Selivanov. Among them was the Squadron's flagship, the venerable cruiser (KR) *Sverdlov*, launched in 1950 as the last all-gun cruiser built in the Soviet Union and in addition to her size, easily recognisable by the bow number of 881. Selivanov personally commanded the *Sverdlov*. He also brought two large anti-submarine warfare ships of the Burevestnik-class with him, with bow numbers 504 and 508. By all accounts, they left port as they were ready, as

A Sverdlov-class cruiser with a submarine tender alongside to port and a Burevestnik/Krivak-class large anti-submarine warfare ship to starboard. Clearly, the *Storozhevoy* was a significantly smaller warship than the *Sverdlov*. (US DoD)

one of the Burevestnik ships, with bow number 508, arrived in the area of operations before the other ships.[4] The pursuit force from Baltiysk arrived too late to participate in the action. When it became clear that it was no longer needed, Selivanov returned to port with his ships.[5]

The boarding team had now taken over the *Storozhevoy*. At about 12:30 p.m., the *Storozhevoy*, at high speed, returned through the Irben Sound, after which she anchored east of the island of Saaremaa at about 15:00 p.m. All the while, until she cast anchor, the two Il-38s kept her under surveillance. The *Storozhevoy* remained there, under guard, until about 11:00 a.m. the next day, when she was escorted to an anchorage north of Riga.

The crew of the *Storozhevoy* was returned to Riga by other ships. The entire crew was interrogated, first by the KGB and then by senior naval officers including Gorshkov himself. Gorshkov treated the conscripts leniently, but he was less forgiving to the officers. Ultimately, Sablin, Shein, and 12 other ringleaders among the mutineers were formally arrested and later taken to Moscow to await trial. The rest of the crew was never prosecuted, certainly to some extent not to exacerbate the crisis but also because Sablin, after he had removed Potul'nyy from the chain of command, was the highest-ranking commander on the warship.

Due to the very serious implications of the suppressed mutiny and the difficulties in finding and attacking the *Storozhevoy*, which showed that the combat readiness of the Soviet Armed Forces was less than desired, the Soviet high command quickly decided to cover up the incident. Having returned to base, Colonel Savinkov and his men were ordered to destroy all documentation of the incident and not tell anybody about it. As far as is known, the other participating air crews received the same order. Instructions to this extent were also issued within the Navy. Yet, discipline was apparently laxer in the naval units. Some officers and crewmen who had participated in the chase certainly discussed it among themselves and also retained some photographs and documents.

Swedish intelligence sources show that rumours eventually surfaced about the mutiny. We will also see that reports based on such rumours were planted in the international press. Nonetheless, Soviet representatives met any rumours and press reports in the Western media that claimed that a mutiny had taken place with denial. Officially, no mutiny had occurred, or even could occur in the Soviet Armed Forces.

8
THE SWEDISH INTELLIGENCE COMMUNITY

The only foreign actor which played a role during the *Storozhevoy* incident – not in the mutiny, but in our understanding of it – was the Swedish intelligence community. By 1975, Sweden maintained an intelligence community which, among its peers abroad, had a long-standing reputation for experience and skill, in particular in signals intelligence (SIGINT). At home, the situation was quite different. In 1973, a disgruntled former intelligence officer and two freelance journalists, one with links to the Soviet KGB, had leaked and exposed in the media major parts of the Swedish intelligence organisational setup. The leak exposed, for the first time, key organisations and personnel within the intelligence community. Because of the exposure, the first Swedish public review of its foreign intelligence community took place in 1974.

For much of the twentieth century, Sweden had adhered to a policy of neutrality. Sweden formally declined to participate in either of the world wars and avoided being a target of any of the belligerent powers. Sweden's intelligence and security services played a major role supporting the country's foreign policy in both the First and particularly the Second World War. It was not by pure chance that Sweden's intelligence system functioned well during the two world wars. Although Sweden had opted out of foreign adventures after the Napoleonic wars, its armed forces possessed an intelligence tradition no less rich than those of the great European powers of long standing. By 1975, Sweden's intelligence services operated in an environment largely formed during the Second World War, but which originated far earlier. The first documented example of Swedish state-controlled military intelligence activities dates back to the Viking Age, c. 1017, and in the sixteenth century Swedish intelligence ran agents in both neighbouring countries and as far away as at the courts of France, England, Spain, and several German states including the Imperial capital of Vienna. Sweden also operated agents in Poland, Muscovy (Russia), and the Tatar Kazan' Khanate on the Volga.[1] The Swedish intelligence system developed yet further during the Thirty Years War of 1618–1648.[2] At an early stage, intelligence activities also included code breaking, and in 1901, within a year of the first Swedish naval experiments in radiotelegraphy, Swedish intelligence began to take an active interest in signals intelligence (SIGINT), with a particular focus on the Russian Baltic Fleet. In 1938, a joint services SIGINT collection unit was set up in the naval base of Karlskrona in southern Sweden. It was named the Defence Staff Radio Establishment (Swedish: *Försvarsstabens radioanstalt*, FRA). With the outbreak of the Second World War, the volume of intercepts increased significantly, and in 1942 prompted the move of the SIGINT service to a new location, outside the capital Stockholm. Reconstituted as an independent authority, known as the National Defence Radio Establishment (*Försvarets radioanstalt*, FRA), under the Ministry of Defence, it continued to report to Section II of the Defence Staff, which was responsible for military intelligence, but henceforth a rapidly increasing volume of reporting also went to the Foreign Ministry, in support of Swedish foreign policy.

An FRA radio direction finding station. (FRA)

During the Cold War, Section II of the Defence Staff continued operations as did the FRA. The wartime clandestine C Bureau (*C-byrån*), responsible for human intelligence (HUMINT), in 1946 reorganised as the T Office (*T-kontoret*). Much of the work henceforth focused on the Soviet threat. In the early days of the Cold War, intelligence on the real circumstances surrounding the Polish people's referendum on 30 June 1946 and parliamentary elections on 19 January 1947 had a particular impact on the Swedish government. The Swedish press trusted the Soviet newspaper *Pravda*, so news reporting presented a rosy picture of the situation. However, SIGINT reporting, based on intercepted Polish cipher telegrams, confirmed the widespread manipulation of the election results and voter intimidation. The FRA reporting enabled the Swedish Prime Minister, Tage Erlander, to assess the real situation in Soviet-controlled Poland and base Sweden's policies on fact, not newspaper reporting. Erlander noted: 'The election methods were exposed with terrible exactness — "investigate so that they do not hide an opposition ballot up their shirtsleeves". So this is the nice election, which even our press has been duped into believing in.'[3] As a result, the FRA reporting greatly influenced the Swedish government's understanding of events in Poland and elsewhere in Soviet-controlled Europe, pushing it further towards the West.

An FRA COMINT station. A chain of such facilities was used to track the movements of the *Storozhevoy* and other warships that took part in the mutiny and resulting actions. (FRA)

The SIGINT effort was not free from loss of life. On 13 June 1952, the service's DC-3 Dakota ELINT aircraft, with an FRA crew, was shot down with no survivors, by a Soviet fighter, while on a mission over the Baltic Sea.

Because of the threat from Soviet agents, Section II of the Defence Staff in 1957 formed a secret counterespionage unit, the B Bureau (*B-byrån*). Technical intelligence organisations were also established which used technical experts from institutions such as the Royal Institute of Technology (*Kungliga tekniska högskolan*, KTH) when, for instance, foreign military materiel had been acquired. In 1945, the Defence Research Establishment (*Försvarets forskningsanstalt*, FOA) was created. The FOA combined the Defence Chemical Establishment (*Försvarsväsendets kemiska anstalt*, FKA), the Institute of Military Physics (*Militärfysiska institutet*, MFI), and a component of the Swedish Board of Inventions (*Statens uppfinnarnämnd*, SUN). The SUN echo radar unit, formed in 1942, was involved in advanced ELINT efforts in addition to research in radar technology. In 1958, at the initiative of Section II of the Defence Staff, intelligence units were formed in the FOA and the service administrations. The latter were reorganised as the Defence Matériel Administration (*Försvarets materielverk*, FMV) in 1968 but retained technical intelligence units.

In 1959 the Eastern Economic Bureau (*Östekonomiska byrån*) was formed with the task to carry out research on the economies of the Soviet bloc. At first a function within the Defence Staff, it was established as a non-state foundation, funded in part from private sources.

The wartime General Security Service was dissolved in 1945, and the National Police resumed responsibility for counterespionage. At the same time, the government severely cut security service funding and staff. It took until the aforementioned Polish elections in early 1947 before the government fully realised that a cold war had begun. Because of the lack of resources and co-ordination, Colonel Stig Wennerström, the spy for the Soviets who perhaps caused most damage to Swedish and other Western interests, successfully operated from at least 1948 until his arrest in 1963. For years, the police and military did not share their suspicions of him.[4]

In 1965, the Swedish police system was finally put under national control. This led to reorganisations also within the military intelligence organisation. The T Office (foreign intelligence) and the B Bureau (counterespionage) were combined, called the IB and subordinated to the head of the Defence Staff. The police were subordinated to a new organisation, called the National Police Board (*Rikspolisstyrelsen*, RPS) which had two departments: the police and the security department. The police department eventually became the National Bureau of Investigation (*Rikskriminalpolisen*, RKP), tasked primarily with organised and transnational crime. The security department (*säkerhetsavdelningen*, SÄK) became responsible for counterespionage.

In 1969, new legislation to safeguard the freedom of opinion outlawed government registration of political sympathies. The RPS claimed sole jurisdiction with regard to domestic security. As a result, the domestic intelligence activities of the IB, primarily counterespionage and the registration of political extremists, ceased in 1970. However, the IB resumed these activities in 1971. As noted above, this was exposed to the media in 1973, together with key organisations and personnel in the intelligence community. The IB's domestic collection again ceased, and in 1974 the first public review of the foreign intelligence community was initiated (a public security service review had taken place already after the Second World War). This was perhaps a first such public review in the Western world; the Swedish review of its foreign intelligence community preceded by a year the establishment in the United States of congressional committees to investigate intelligence community transgressions revealed by the press. Henceforth, all foreign intelligence activities were also put under direct government and parliamentary oversight with the establishment of the Defence Intelligence Committee (*Försvarets Underrättelsenämnd*, FUN).

No longer permitted to engage in domestic intelligence activities, the IB was reorganised in 1973 and renamed the Joint Intelligence Bureau (*Gemensamma byrån för underrättelser*, GBU). The change in name was so secret that many of the organisation's officers were unaware of it and continued to describe the agency as the IB.

Nonetheless, Swedish foreign intelligence remained both active and able, and a major part of the national intelligence collection effort was handled by the SIGINT agency, the FRA.

Even so, on Sunday 9 November 1975 no officer, at least no senior one, within the Swedish intelligence community yet knew any details about the dramatic events which unfolded around the *Storozhevoy* just east of the island of Gotland. The intelligence services of the NATO member states knew even less, in most or all cases not even realising that some unusual activity had taken place.

The Intelligence Reporting

Although the mutiny was monitored and recorded in real-time, it took some time before the Swedish SIGINT service reacted to the unexpected seriousness of the situation. The mutiny took place on a Saturday night and the search for the *Storozhevoy* was carried out on a Sunday. At that time, Swedish intelligence personnel were not normally on duty on weekends. Although some intelligence personnel, including FRA SIGINT collectors, worked shifts, outside office hours there was no one who processed and analysed the

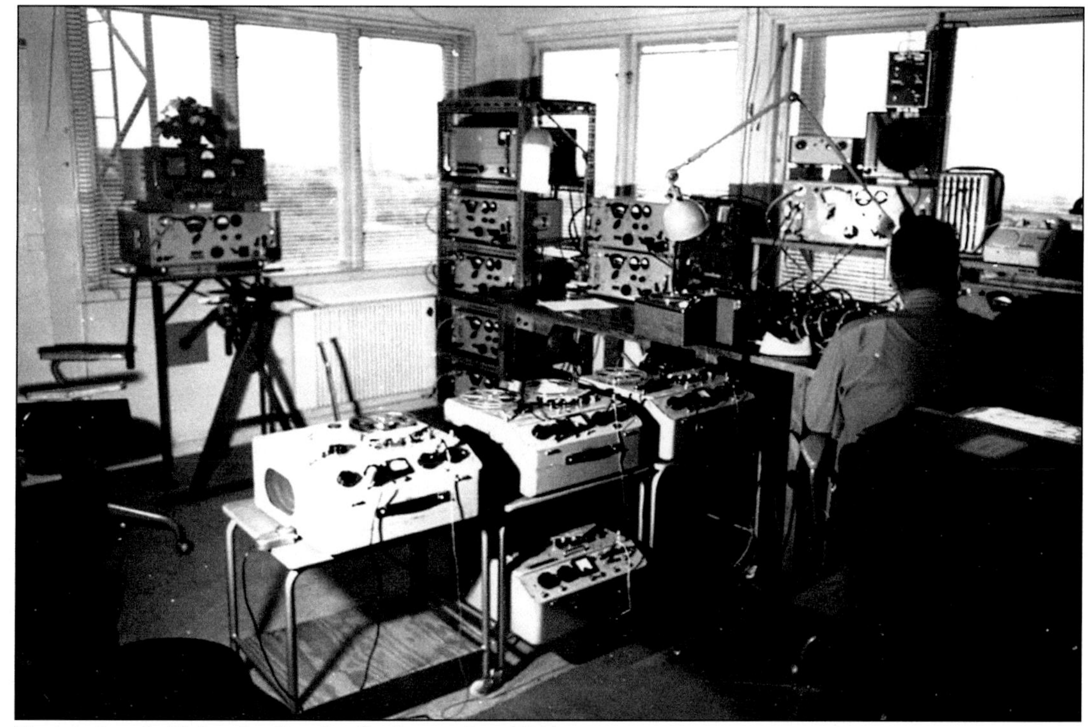

The interior of a FRA radio direction finding station. (FRA)

The interior of a COMINT station of the FRA. (FRA)

of the Burevestnik-class) was, the report noted, an 'unusual activity'.

During the afternoon this Monday, processing and analysis of the collected intercepts continued at FRA headquarters, and just before the end of the working day, the finished report, with all details, was sent to the Navy Staff and Air Force Staff. The report built further on the information in the previous summary and stated, among other things, that on Sunday 9 November a ship force consisting of about 10 units (more had now been identified) had co-exercised with Naval Aviation aircraft and about 20 aircraft from Tukums Air Base. The *Storozhevoy* had then returned into the Gulf of Riga. On the same day, Sunday 9 November, other Naval Aviation aircraft too had also operated in the area. Six aircraft from Bykhov Air Base had stayed in the area, where they had been found to be circling for some time, from the morning to the early afternoon (Moscow time). At the same time, two anti-submarine warfare aircraft from Riga Skulte Air Base had exercised with the *Storozhevoy* and *Komsomolets Litvy* during the morning and the early afternoon (Moscow time).

The report also stated that the *Storozhevoy* was 'possibly attacked' by aircraft from Tukums Air Base – but since this was only noted in connection with the aviation operation, and the description of the naval operation repeatedly referred to a 'joint exercise', no one seems to have seriously considered the possibility that the attack was carried out with sharp weapons. There may have been some suspicion of the latter among the SIGINT collectors who monitored the radio traffic from the aviation units.[5] That traffic was in plain text and was picked up by staff who had a solid knowledge of Russian. These may well have reacted to the fact that the radio communications on the day in question were markedly different compared to the usual ones. But even if this was the case, and no documentation of it seems to have been preserved in the FRA archive, in any case that idea was dismissed when a synthesis of the various intercept reports was made and the summary of the course of events was written. The compilation was written by staff at FRA headquarters on Lovön Island and was based on the written reporting from the SIGINT collectors. Those who compiled the report were personnel who did not necessarily take in the suspicions of the collectors, did not always know Russian, and to them the idea that a live attack would have taken place probably seemed completely irrational. This was not part of the normal picture, so the possibility of this happening was quickly written off – if it was even considered.

When the reports from the FRA (formally the two parts were considered one daily report, even though the summary was sent first and the details only towards the end of the afternoon) reached the Navy Staff and the Air Force Staff, they did not cause any stir. There is nothing to suggest that the Navy Staff paid any special attention to the reports on the day in question. However, a certain interest was aroused in the Air Force Staff. Within the radar intelligence service, which was then located at the Air Force Staff, it was noted – either

intercepts obtained. So, on Monday 10 November, the collected intercepts from the weekend were compiled at FRA headquarters on Lovön Island, near Stockholm. The results were then reported to the intelligence and security departments of the Navy and Air Force Staff, respectively. Thence, it was assumed that the information would be forwarded also to the military intelligence service of the Defence Staff.

The first report – a summary – was sent immediately after lunch. The report dealt with everything that happened from 8:00 a.m. on Friday 7 November to 8:00 a.m. on Monday 10 November. It always took a few hours to compile the weekend's events. The report stated, among other matters, that a fleet of at least eight Soviet warships, including the *Storozhevoy*, on Sunday 9 November had exercised with Naval Aviation aircraft and Frontal Aviation aircraft from Tukums Air Base in the area west – west-southwest of the island of Saaremaa. The *Storozhevoy* had then passed into the Gulf of Riga. That aircraft from the Frontal Aviation regiment at Tukums 'co-exercised' with a missile destroyer (as we have seen, the then Western designation

Wilhelm Agrell. (Agrell Collection)

from the FRA's report or through the analysts' own examination of the radar images – that something unusual had happened. There were several capable analysts within the service, including a couple of young, fairly new employees. One of them, Ulf Hugo, had by then been with the radar intelligence service for a few months. He had begun work at the Swedish Air Force's Intelligence and Security Department in 1973. Another, Wilhelm Agrell, had been hired in 1974. At the Air Force's Intelligence and Security Department's section for tactics assessment, he was responsible for the analytical monitoring of Soviet Frontal Aviation in the Baltic Military District. When on Monday Wilhelm Agrell met Ulf Hugo in passing in the corridor, the latter mentioned that 'your Brewers have been out and carried out a bombing'.[6] In his hand, Ulf Hugo carried the first of today's reports from the FRA, the summary, which had noted 'unusual activity'.[7]

Agrell later described the situation as follows:

> By *my Brewers* he meant one of the light bomber regiments. . . Over time, an almost intimate familiarity developed with the units on the other side, their exercises, daily routines, and managerial concerns.
>
> My Brewers. . . had thus been out dropping bombs, which was a natural thing for them since they were a bomber unit. However, there were two circumstances that were a bit different and that was why my colleague had raised the issue. The first was that they flew on a Sunday morning, the second and perhaps more interesting was that they practised bombing against targets at sea. The possibility of such efforts on the part of Frontal Aviation units was one of the issues discussed among intelligence analysts on the aviation side. Given the geostrategic conditions in the Baltic Sea region, the matter was of great importance; Tactical air operations would entail an increase and change in the air threat against Swedish naval forces and thus indirectly affect Sweden's air defence capability.
>
> But apart from this, I did not pay much attention to the event itself as such. The intended enemy always had ongoing activities on the other side of the Baltic Sea and this was a week like any other, with the routinely repeated conclusion *no signs of a heightened state of alert among foreign forces in the immediate area*. I was waiting to see if there would be more and similar exercises, which could indicate a changed pattern.[8]

The radar intelligence service had undeniably noted that a number of Yak-28s from a Frontal Aviation regiment had appeared over the sea west of the Latvian town of Ventspils.[9] They had been identified by the FRA, but judging by the information available, it was unclear to the Swedes what kind of activity they had actually carried out over there. The aircraft had first flown at low altitude, so it was really only the return flight that with some form of clarity could be observed by Swedish radar. There had also been no electronic warfare (EW) interference, and such were common in larger exercises. The assessment was made that the aircraft possibly carried out some form of attack on the naval task force, which was in the area, but that assessment was apparently solely made on the basis of the FRA's report. The possibility was cautiously noted that the whole operation, especially compared to the very low flight activity earlier in the week due to the celebration of the Day of the Great October Socialist Revolution, could be some form of control of the level of combat alert within the Soviet units.

On Tuesday 11 November, the processing and analysis continued at the FRA. At lunchtime, as on all weekdays, a summary of the events of the past 24 hours was sent to those who received the agency's reporting. The summary pointed out, among other things, that the *Storozhevoy* was now in the Gulf of Riga. At the same time, the incident on Sunday had not been completely forgotten. In the detailed report which followed during the afternoon, it was noted that of the Soviet naval task force mentioned yesterday, the majority of ships had probably now entered the Gulf of Riga. It was then acknowledged that the activities conducted on Sunday could not be identified. At the FRA's headquarters on Lovön Island, they simply did not yet know what had happened.

However, signals intelligence and radar intelligence were not the only Swedish sources of intelligence. After the mutineers on the *Storozhevoy* surrendered on Sunday 9 November, she had been escorted back into the Gulf of Riga, where she spent the night at anchor. On Monday morning, the *Storozhevoy* was escorted to a position in the Gulf of Riga north of the port of Riga, where she remained until 17 November. But some of the ships that had escorted the *Storozhevoy* back into Soviet waters continued into the port of Riga, where they docked that evening. As mentioned, the *Komsomolets Litvy* had been damaged during the air attack, and when she moved into the harbour for repairs, rumour soon spread among the dockyard workers that something unusual had happened.

It did not happen every day that a warship with combat damage came in for repairs. Among the dockyard workers was one who had a special interest in the issue, as he worked for the Swedish intelligence service. The dockyard worker had a secure communication channel to a contact in a third country, and he informed his contact that a warship with combat damage had been brought into port. The contact in turn had a communication channel to a man in Sweden named Alex Milits (1932–2012), who was thus informed of the incident. Milits worked for the GBU, the Swedish HUMINT service. As noted, the old organisational name IB had been compromised through a media leak, so the organisation had for two years been renamed the GBU, even though many of its employees still used the old name IB. Milits had come from Estonia to Sweden in 1944, at the age of 12. He lived in Tullinge south of Stockholm and also worked as a journalist. Like many Balts, who saw the Soviet empire subjugate their homelands, Milits had volunteered to work for Swedish intelligence. Milits had a previously planned meeting with

Jan Leijonhielm. (Leijonhielm Collection)

Alex Milits. (Milits Collection)

the GBU case officer Jan Leijonhielm (b. 1944). When the two met on Wednesday 19 November, Milits took the opportunity to ask Leijonhielm what they had learned about the mutiny within the Soviet Baltic Fleet. For understandable reasons, Leijonhielm did not know about the incident, which nobody had yet identified at central level either in Stockholm or on Lovön Island. So Milits told what he knew, which at that time was not much more than what the dockyard worker had reported. Milits had simply taken for granted that Swedish intelligence already knew what had happened. Leijonhielm urged Milits to inquire about more details from his sources, and later in the week Milits returned by phone with more information.[10] Leijonhielm immediately afterwards wrote a report on the incident, which was communicated to the Navy Staff.

So, by the end of November 1975, the Swedish intelligence community had begun to get a picture of what had taken place. However, there was still uncertainty about major chunks of the course of events. In addition, there was not yet any version of the event in which intelligence from different sources had been fused. Each agency had its information, and no attempt had yet been made to clarify the general course of events. And which agency would do that? The Navy Staff? The Air Force Staff? The Defence Staff? The GBU? The FRA?

Nor does any fusion of the various intelligence sources appear to have been made until the mass media intervened in the process. Or, to clarify the situation, before an intelligence source took up the track in his regular work as a journalist.

The Mass Media Effect

On 22 January 1976, the Swedish tabloid *Expressen* published a long article about the mutiny. The article had been written by Milits, who routinely worked as a journalist, and it was stated to be based on information from 'Latvian fishermen', who had happened to be in the area, and from 'several foreign tourists' who had returned from Riga. The vague information in the *Expressen* was of course due to the fact that Milits needed to protect his real sources.

Milits later explained, but before he went public with his connection to Swedish intelligence, that he had found out about the incident from a Latvian who had just visited Riga and had been told that a mutiny had taken place on a large warship, which his Latvian source had been unable to identify. Milits then said that he had made enquiries among Baltic sailors in the port of Stockholm, after which an anonymous man called him by phone to tell that a warship in Riga had been damaged by bombs during the hunt for the mutineer. Milits then said that he had asked for the name of the ship on which the mutiny had taken place. The anonymous source had reportedly answered '*Storozhevoy*' and then hung up without waiting for more questions. Milits therefore said that he had misunderstood the identity of the ship. As we have seen, the Russian term "*storozhevoy korabl*'" by this time meant a patrol ship such as the *Komsomolets Litvy*, or possibly the yet smaller border guard ships of the Project 205P Tarantul class of the Border Troops, which suggested something much smaller than a large anti-submarine warfare ship such as the *Storozhevoy*.[11]

It was perhaps the article in the tabloid *Expressen* that made other Western intelligence services open their eyes to the incident. The American Naval Attaché in Stockholm in the period 1974–1976, Captain Thomas Wheeler, reported on 29 January 1976 that a mutiny may have taken place on a Soviet warship. At the American embassy in Stockholm, however, they were not even sure that anything had happened. According to Wheeler, there was also no US intelligence information about the incident. The radar station on Bornholm Island, Denmark, could contribute some fragmentary information, he said, but due to the large distance, that radar station could not have observed much, if anything, of the course of events surrounding the mutiny and the subsequent hunt for the *Storozhevoy*. There were no US intelligence assets in the region at the time. For sure, U.S. Navy reconnaissance aircraft often flew over the Baltic Sea, in particular when the Swedes had tipped them off that new Soviet warships or aircraft carried out final tests there (in comparison, the US Strategic Air Command solely focused on the Soviet air defence capabilities). But this time, the mutiny had come as a surprise to everybody, so there had been no tip-off. The American attaché report also included a copy of Milits's article in the *Expressen*, which says something about Wheeler's lack of access to information. Little did Wheeler know that Milits worked for Swedish intelligence! But Wheeler knew that signals intelligence information existed and could be used to identify the ship on which the mutiny had taken place. The *Storozhevoy*'s bow number was mentioned in Wheeler's report.[12] As far as can be judged in retrospect, it was the

Swedish Defence Staff which almost certainly gave that information to Wheeler, even though it ultimately stemmed from the original reporting to the Navy Staff from the FRA.

At that time, the FRA was already reprocessing the intercepted radio traffic. The work was carried out by Rune Axelsson (1922–1988), a very experienced naval analyst who had already served a quarter of a century at the FRA, since 1951. Axelsson had solid knowledge of the Soviet Navy and had monitored its operations for decades. On 11 February 1976, his work resulted in a report on the mutiny and its aftermath. The report, disseminated to the intelligence functions of the Defence Staff, Navy Staff, and Air Force Staff, was described as a preliminary compilation. It is unknown when work on it began. Relatively much recorded radio traffic, however, seems to have been analysed, so even though the work on the specific report to the Defence Staff may have started as a direct result of the article in the *Expressen*, there is much to suggest that the post-processing work of the intercepts already was in full swing when the article in the *Expressen* was published. And although the report was described as a preliminary compilation, it contained a good description of the military aspects of the course of events surrounding the mutiny – in fact a better and factually more correct one than the many books and TV documentaries that were published much later. The reason was not necessarily that the FRA's analysts were better than the journalists and writers who eventually began to look into the event (although Rune Axelsson probably was). More importantly, they worked with the radio traffic exactly as it unfolded at the time, unlike recent writers and filmmakers who had to rely on second-hand sources or personal reminiscences that had sometimes changed over time. From a source-criticism perspective, the authenticity, independence, and contemporaneity of the radio traffic intercepts were what made the FRA's material the most credible of the available sources. (This also applies to later historians, since the FRA's materials, especially in terms of chronology, have the character of a remnant rather than a narrative source, which gives it higher credibility.)

The FRA's report was followed on 8 March 1976 by an intelligence report on the incident prepared by the Defence Staff.[13] This intelligence report was almost entirely based on the report from the FRA, except that it also referred to the information from Milits that at least one pursuing ship had been accidentally damaged by a free-fall bomb attack.[14] The report, however, also mentioned the article in the Soviet military daily *Krasnaya zvezda* on 24 December 1974, which pointed out shortcomings in political education and motivation on board the *Storozhevoy*. That reference also came from Milits and shows that the Defence Staff finally had at least an idea of what the mutiny had ultimately been about.[15]

And with that, the intelligence community's focus on the mutiny on the *Storozhevoy* was largely over. The big questions had been answered. It was known on which ship the mutiny had taken place, and how it had all unfolded. The personal names of the officers involved were not yet known, nor the fate that befell them. But in all honesty, these details were not part of Sweden's need for intelligence about the Soviet Union. The incident was already over, and Sweden had not been affected by it. The situation would have been different if the *Storozhevoy* had entered Swedish waters, but that was never the case. For the Swedish intelligence community, the slowness in identifying the course of events was a sign of shortcomings in how the operation was conducted, but the mutiny on the *Storozhevoy* was never an intelligence failure in its usual meaning – because the incident had no real consequences for Swedish action or policy.

It may nevertheless be of interest to describe a few more details of the mass media effect. On 4 May 1976, the tabloid *Expressen* published another article about the *Storozhevoy*. This article, too, was written by Milits, and this time the information in the tabloid was both more detailed and factually accurate.[16] Now the daily *Svenska Dagbladet* also caught on and on the following day repeated the *Expressen*'s information, but – feeling the need also to have something new to bring into the picture – with the addition that a spokesman for the Defence Staff on the day before, that is, Tuesday 4 May, had told the newspaper's journalist Curt Jonasson that the FRA followed the drama of the *Storozhevoy* mutiny and recorded some of the radio traffic. The FRA's name was thus used as a way to compete with the other newspapers' information. The *Svenska Dagbladet* nevertheless tried to hide the sources of the intelligence service, but without much success: 'Sources of information are also assumed to be, for example, various Baltic exile organisations, but above all the intelligence collection conducted in the Baltic Sea region, among others by Sweden, mainly through radio intercepts.'[17] However, that was not the end of the matter. Since the *Svenska Dagbladet* now had a contact in the Defence Staff who was willing to talk about the *Storozhevoy* mutiny, the newspaper also published a follow-up article nine days later. This time, the daily could report that the crew of a Tu-16K bomber had refused to attack the *Storozhevoy*. Although the detailed information about the radar malfunction in Colonel Savinkov's Tu-16K bomber was not revealed, it was this information that later spread a false narrative that some Soviet pilots refused to attack the mutineers.[18]

The Remaining Question

> Combat readiness is no motto or high-flown phrase, but a totally concrete concept. It is that state of the Armed Forces in which they are capable of repelling and disrupting aggression at any moment and under the most difficult conditions of the situation, no matter what the source or the means and methods used, including nuclear weapons.[19]

This is how the Marshal of the Soviet Union, Andrey Grechko, described the meaning of combat readiness in the Soviet military. The quote is of interest, as Grechko, in his capacity as defence minister, apparently was the one who woke up the Soviet Union's supreme leader, Brezhnev, on the morning of 9 November to inform him about the mutiny. Grechko had also personally visited the *Storozhevoy* the autumn before, a visit that gave rise to the article in the *Krasnaya Zvezda* on 24 December of the same year in which the lack of discipline on board the warship was criticised. It was also Grechko who ordered the 668th Bomber Aviation Regiment from Tukums Air Base to attack the *Storozhevoy*.

Why did Grechko choose that particular bomber aviation regiment? Tukums Air Base was, of course, geographically close to the area of operation and surely bombing was seen as a way to threaten the mutineers to give up. At the same time, the question can be asked: If the purpose now was to sink the *Storozhevoy* rather than let her get away, why did he not use the Tu-16K bomber's anti-ship missiles from the outset? Colonel Savinkov's Tu-16K bomber was already in place and an experienced officer like Grechko should have foreseen the difficulties for the Yak-28 pilots to carry out the attack. However, the choice of air unit may have been due to Grechko's realisation that the Tu-16K bomber's payload was catastrophically unsuitable for an operation of this kind.

After the *Storozhevoy* incident, the young intelligence analyst Agrell particularly pondered one question about the course of events surrounding the mutiny on the *Storozhevoy*. The Yak-28s had not been the first to attack the warship. The Tu-16K bombers had then already attacked the *Storozhevoy* with automatic cannon fire. However, the mutineers had not given up. Finally, the Tu-16K bomber commander had received the order to 'Use the weapon'. At the FRA, the intercept analysts assessed that the 'weapon' referred to an anti-ship missile. However, the Tu-16K bomber commander reported a radar malfunction before any missile launch took place. He therefore ordered the other two Tu-16K bombers to attack independently.

There is no information in the FRA archive that the FRA analysts pondered further about what kind of weapon the Tu-16K bombers had prepared to deploy. The missile launch was stopped at the last moment. But the question was highly relevant, and Agrell wondered what kind of weapon it might have been. In addition to its automatic cannons for self-defence use, the Tu-16K bomber of the type in question was normally only armed with a single anti-ship missile which employed radar to lock on the target. The problem was that it came in two variants, one loaded with a conventional warhead and another, probably the more common type, loaded with a nuclear warhead. The interception of mutineers was not any regular task of either Naval Aviation or the Tu-16K bombers. Under normal conditions, we have seen that the primary target of Naval Aviation Tu-16K bombers would have been an American aircraft carrier group, and to destroy a carrier required significantly stronger weapons than a single conventional warhead.

The Tu-16K bombers had taken off early in the morning during a weekend. A reasonable assumption was that they constituted the contingent on combat alert duty, which was always ready for immediate response in the event of a sudden nuclear attack on the Soviet Union. And in the event of such an attack, it was no doubt that nuclear weapons would be deployed when Tu-16K bombers were ordered into the air to counter the enemy attack. Had the Tu-16K bombers in question been armed with nuclear weapons this time, too, and was the weapons launch that was interrupted at the last moment really a nuclear attack against the *Storozhevoy*? This would undoubtedly have been a decisive, last resort to ensure that the mutineers and their ships never reached Swedish waters. But such an attack would also have resulted in a nuclear explosion only about 100km east of northern Gotland.

Now, of course, the *Storozhevoy* was not an American aircraft carrier, and the Soviet leadership knew that World War III had not broken out. But that does not prevent the Tu-16K bombers, which were on standby that night, from having been armed with appropriate weapons. And the logical alternative, if it was a sudden counterattack against an American aircraft carrier group that was planned for, was anti-ship missiles with nuclear warheads. The Tu-16K bombers in question also took off in groups of three, which directly corresponded to the doctrine's emphasis on firing volleys of nuclear missiles in groups of three. Did they have time to change the weapons load at the air base before the mission began? That is far from certain.

As for the second air regiment which was deployed this early morning, the 668th Bomber Aviation Regiment at Tukums Air Base, we know that the aircraft carried the wrong weapons load. Since the regiment's expected task in war was to attack enemy air bases, the prepared weapons load consisted of 250kg free-fall fragmentation bombs. The commander of the regiment realised, of course, that against a ship target it would be much more effective to use 500kg high-explosive bombs. Such armaments existed on base, but they were locked away in another storage depot. And when uncertainty about what type of bomb to deploy was greatest, as mentioned, the commander of the 15th Tactical Air Army, Major General Gvozdikov, suddenly called personally to give tactical instructions on how to carry out the attack. Gvozdikov ordered the regiment *not* to change the already prepared weapons load, as it was urgent to take off.[20] So the bombers took off with the original bomb load, which was intended for strikes on enemy air bases. Maybe it was lucky, because as a result no one was injured or killed on the ships that were then bombed. But the order was already then to prepare to *sink* the *Storozhevoy*, and for that the weapons load should have been different.

Are there any corresponding testimonies from the Tu-16K bomber pilots who were present? Some of the former pilots of the 57th Bomber Aviation Division remember Colonel Savinkov and the course of events surrounding the ordered launch of anti-ship missiles. They can confirm that the commander of Naval Aviation of the Baltic Fleet, Colonel General Gulyayev, ordered the launch and also confirmed the launch order by the special protocol for the launch of nuclear missiles. One of them, who in 1975 belonged to the Division but had not himself participated in the mission, explained the following about how the launch was ordered: 'There were assigned – two numbers. Those who are in the know will understand. I do not need to explain further.'[21] Why, then, had all the ships been ordered to move away at least 10km from the *Storozhevoy*? Was it because the warhead was not a conventional charge? The former pilot said, however, that it was still a conventional warhead, and that the safety distance ordered was only due to the fact that the anti-ship missiles of this type did not always steer correctly, which was already known at the time the doctrine was written. He was sure of his case. Colonel Savinkov had taken off with an anti-ship missile with a conventional warhead.

However, there is conflicting information as to why Colonel Savinkov did not fire the anti-ship missile. According to the former pilots' recent testimony, this was due to the fact that they had already come too close to the *Storozhevoy* and that the missile would therefore not have been able to lock on to and hit the target. At the same time, one of the veteran pilots commented on the incident with the following words about his former commander: 'Savinkov was a good officer who knew that it was not always wise to follow orders, in particular when the consequences of obeying were impossible to know.'[22]

This could indicate that Savinkov faked his radar malfunction so as not to have to fire. But why did he then immediately afterwards order the other Tu-16K bombers to carry out the attack? Could the cohesion in the group have been such that they jointly agreed not to launch their weapons? In an interview much later, Colonel Gulyayev hinted that this was the case.[23] Or, is the recent discussion a post-fact reconstruction? After all, was it only a radar malfunction and the subsequent cease-fire command that prevented the launch?

Yet another possibility, more plausible but like the others one that cannot be verified based on the surviving and available materials, is that Savinkov's unit carried a mixed weapons load. In this case, Savinkov's own aircraft carried the missile with a nuclear warhead, while the other two aircraft in his unit carried missiles with conventional warheads.[24] A mixed weapons load corresponded to Soviet doctrine and would explain why Savinkov did not launch his missile, yet ordered his subordinates to continue the operation and carry out the attack.

On the basis of the available materials, it is not possible to determine with absolute certainty what kind of weapons load the Tu-16K bombers in question carried on the day of the mutiny. That question can probably only be answered through Soviet archives, in case the information is still there and has not been destroyed, which is said to have been the case with the documentation from the 668th Bomber Aviation Regiment.[25] The documentation from the 240th Guard Bomber Aviation Regiment may also have been deliberately distorted. One of the navigation officers of the regiment, now deceased, wrote in his flight log that he participated in an exercise on the day in question. However, the time and other details are consistent with the operation against the *Storozhevoy*, so the late navigation officer's family suspects that he may have been part of Savinkov's unit.[26] Could it be that after the mission, other officers in the 57th Bomber Aviation Division were deliberately given the wrong information about the weapons load? None of these pilots had himself been involved in the mission.

That the contingent on combat alert duty normally carried nuclear weapons is an assumption that cannot be proven. However, there is an indication that the ordered weapons launch was in fact considered to be of much higher dignity than automatic machine gun firing and bombing. It was not the unit commander in the air who ultimately ordered the deployment of the 'weapon'. This was done by the commander of Naval Aviation of the Baltic Fleet, Colonel General Gulyayev, who himself may have been in a specially equipped command and control aircraft, from which he first ordered weapons launch, and also employed the special protocol for the launch of nuclear missiles. This was noted by the FRA, but the details only emerged during the post-processing of the intercepts. When the FRA's final report eventually was issued, in February 1976, the event was too far back in time to attract much attention. However, even this is only an indication that a nuclear attack may have been intended. The situation with the mutiny was so remarkable in itself that, for this very reason, the Soviet leadership may have used extraordinary procedures to secure control of the loyal units.

Yet, the available evidence, taken together, still suggests that the Soviet leadership ordered a nuclear missile attack on the *Storozhevoy*, and that Vice Admiral Kosov and Colonel General Gulyayev both in turn passed on the order to Colonel Savinkov. The remaining evidence certainly suggests that at least Savinkov's bomber carried a missile with a nuclear warhead. First, SIGINT reveals that Savinkov executed the special protocol for launching a nuclear missile. Second, Savinkov and his men had been on standard combat alert at the time. Their intended target, if war had broken out, would have been a US carrier group. For such a target, nuclear-armed missiles would have been used. Furthermore, there is reason to believe that the radar failure reported by Savinkov was a subterfuge so as to avoid the launching of a nuclear missile. That he then nonetheless ordered the other two bombers to launch may indicate that while Savinkov carried a nuclear-armed missile, the other two Tu-16Ks did not. In the final assessment, it can only be concluded that evidence suggests that the Soviet command ordered a nuclear attack, but that conclusive evidence remains unavailable. Brezhnev, Grechko, Gorshkov, Kosov, Gulyayev, and Savinkov have all passed away, while those who participated in the operation and remain with us today are still reluctant to speak about it.

To conclude, even if there is no unequivocal evidence, the possibility remains that a nuclear attack just east of Gotland may have been ordered on 9 November 1975, no matter how unlikely this may seem. Fortunately, the radar on the bomber in question malfunctioned, or was claimed to have malfunctioned, so the anti-ship missile could not be launched. For another critical minute, the two other Tu-16K bombers prepared attacks with their missiles, but before any launch could take place, their commander ordered the attack to be aborted.

For about two minutes around 10.45 a.m., many lives hung on a fragile thread. This was especially true of Sablin, Shein, Potul'nyy, and the other imprisoned officers and crew as well as the mutineers. Many of them would have been killed if the *Storozhevoy* had been sunk by an anti-ship missile. If the missile on Savinkov's Tu-16K bomber that day was loaded with a nuclear warhead, many Soviet sailors and pilots in the pursuit force as well as an unknown number of Gotlanders, Balts, and Russians living along the Baltic coast would also have been at risk. As the veteran of the 57th Bomber Aviation Division put it, it is not always wise to obey orders, especially if the consequences of obeying are impossible to predict.

9
CONSEQUENCES OF THE MUTINY

Sablin was an idealist. He failed to anticipate the likely outcome of his grandiose venture. To realise his vision, he was willing to sacrifice his own life, as well as his wife Nina and son Mikhail. Of course, the latter were not on board, but none of them could expect a bright future in the Soviet Union with a traitor in the family. It was not only his wife and son who suffered. He also caused grief to his parents, who soon passed away, and difficulties for his brothers, who like Nina and Mikhail had to live with a traitor in the family. Shein suffered, too, and even though he supported their actions during the trial, it seems abundantly clear that he would not have incited a mutiny on his own, had he not been subject to Sablin's persuasive powers.

Today, there are devout Marxists inside and outside Russia who praise Sablin as a hero. For them, it does not matter that Sablin was also prepared to sacrifice the lives of a couple of hundred crew members of the *Storozhevoy*. These men had families, too, whose lives were in danger of being destroyed. The same can be said about the risk to the Soviet sailors in the interception force. And the possible consequences if the mutiny had caused an international crisis are impossible to assess. Sablin did not care about this. For him, the socialist revolution was the only thing that mattered. His grandiose personality and self-centred vision prevented him from making a realistic assessment of what he set out to do.

These aspects of Sablin's personality were also evident in his make-believe Revolutionary Committee. Not only was no such committee ever formed, except in Sablin's imagination. He had also drawn up plans for a yet more elaborate revolutionary structure, with an organisation he, in a fantasy, had named the Ship's Revolutionary Forces (*Revolyutsionnyye sily korablya*, RSK). This would supposedly be a union of like-minded activists who wanted to participate in communist revolutionary education in order to create a mass movement throughout the Soviet Union and establish a centre for political activities. However, even more striking than this grandiose vision was the way Sablin envisioned the leadership of the RSK. He would pick 12 supporters who with himself as the 13th member would function as the general assembly of the movement. Meeting weekly, Sablin and his 12 followers would make decisions on future activities. Each member of the general assembly would have one vote, except Sablin who would have two.[1] It is hard to escape the feeling that Sablin's vision was close to a communist version of the first Christians, with Sablin himself as Christ and the followers as his apostles.

Having considered these hard facts, we should still, with the benefit of hindsight, at least credit Sablin with correctly identifying the problems in Soviet society. In what he had intended to be his open radio broadcast, Sablin argued that it was necessary 'openly to address a range of questions about the political, social, and economic development of our country, about the future of our people, requiring collective, namely, nationwide discussion without pressure from government or party organs'. Only a decade after the mutiny on the *Storozhevoy*, the then new supreme leader of the Soviet Union, Mikhail Gorbachev, initiated the perestroika and glasnost policies as means to reform Soviet society. What Gorbachev called for was essentially the future that Sablin had dreamt of, and with these policies, Gorbachev opened up for discussion the very issues that Sablin had raised. Sablin was not only a dangerous idealist whose reckless actions almost caused the detonation of a probably nuclear warhead; he was also a predecessor of Gorbachev's reform policies. These policies, in hindsight necessary for Soviet society but in their short-term application almost as reckless as Sablin's actions, led to the unintended dissolution of the Soviet Union. This was not a process free from violence but it set post-Soviet space on the path to a better future with significantly more freedoms, including democratic elections, and a higher quality of life than Soviet socialism ever could have provided.

Did Sablin's ambitious plan have any chance of success? Obviously, he thought so. But when that did not happen, Sablin still thought that he would be pardoned.[2] Perhaps he really believed in the hollow but Party-mandated description of the Soviet soldier which the Minister of Defence, Marshal Grechko, had used to conclude his well-known book about the Soviet armed forces:

> ...[the Soviet soldier] possesses high moral-combat qualities. The Communist Party has armed him with invincible revolutionary Marxist-Leninist teachings which contain an inexhaustible source of ideological maturity and communist conviction of all personnel of the Armed Forces. Our people can be sure that today's generation of Soviet soldiers are worthy heirs and continuers of the revolutionary, combat, and labor traditions of their grandfathers and fathers and true guardians of the Party and people, ready to stand up staunchly in defence of the Socialist Motherland.[3]

Nobody could deny that Sablin was a revolutionary Marxist-Leninist and perhaps he regarded the name of *Storozhevoy* (usually translated as 'Sentry' but the term could just as easily mean 'Guardian') as symbolic of what he attempted to do to save the Socialist Motherland. If so, perhaps he thought that he deserved a pardon. Yet, this did not happen.

Of all the mutineers, only Sablin and Shein were charged with serious crimes. The other men who had been identified as ringleaders were charged only with insubordination, not treason. Insubordination merited disciplinary sanctions but not a criminal charge. No doubt, Shein would have been excluded from prosecution for treason, too, had he not gone out of his way to declare his support for Sablin and the righteousness of the aim of the mutiny to topple the Soviet government. Shein was sentenced to eight years in prison and labour camp. Sablin was sentenced to death and executed on 3 August 1976, the only one who lost his life in connection with the mutiny.[4]

If any of the participants in the events surrounding the mutiny on the *Storozhevoy* should be singled out as the true guardian of the people and the Motherland, this honour would instead seem to belong to Colonel Savinkov. He had shown himself ready to act against the mutineers, but as we have seen, not with the launch of a nuclear-armed missile, as he apparently was ordered, but through the use of missiles with conventional warheads, which he ordered his team to launch. However, the implicit refusal to launch what probably was a nuclear warhead so close to the Motherland paradoxically meant that Savinkov spent the rest of his career under the cloud of suspicion. His superior, Colonel General Gulyayev, clearly regarded Savinkov as a traitor who refused to follow orders during a national emergency.[5]

We have seen that Gorshkov and the other senior naval officers treated the conscripts among the mutineers with lenience during interrogations. The interrogations formed part of the work of the military commission, with Admiral Gorshkov as chairman, which the Minister of Defence, Marshal Grechko, established to investigate the mutiny on the *Storozhevoy*.

On 17 November 1975, the military commission issued its report on the mutiny to the Minister of Defence. The committee, which had concluded its work on 14 November, included several senior admirals and generals. Addressing the Minister of Defence, Gorshkov and his colleagues reported that:

> The commission, created by your order No. 00105 of 9 November 1975, has concluded its investigation into the case of insubordination which took place on 8–9 November this year on the large anti-submarine warfare ship *Storozhevoy*, 128th Missile Ship Brigade of the Baltic Fleet.
>
> On the ship were 194 people. Among them: 15 officers, 14 warrant officers, 165 petty officers and sailors; 7 members of the Communist Party of the Soviet Union, 9 candidate members of the Communist Party of the Soviet Union, 164 Komsomol [Young Communist League] members. The crew included representatives of 18 nationalities, including: 111 Russians, 22 Ukrainians, 12 Belarusians, 5 Latvians, 5 Moldavians, 3 Lithuanians, 2 Poles, and others. By social class: 114 workers, 19 peasants, 29 office workers, 32 students.
>
> The ship's unauthorized departure to sea and disobedience to command were the result of the criminal activities of the former political officer SABLIN, a malevolent anti-Soviet degenerate, hiding behind the uniform of an officer who, through demagogic statements and deception, managed to temporarily win over some of the ship's crew to his side.
>
> The extraordinary incident was also the result of the ill-judged activities of a certain group of people who succumbed to the demagogic, deceitful agitation of the enemy, who over an extended period of time nurtured criminal intentions towards the existing order in the party and our state. Invoking the high authority of his position, knowing the psychology of many of his subordinates, subtly playing on their feelings, and distorting

facts, SABLIN succeeded in persuading the psychologically unstable part of the crew that he only wanted publicly to criticise shortcomings in the political, social, and economic development of our country.

An examination of SABLIN's personal notes, other materials prepared by him, and his behaviour during the investigation allow us to characterise him as a man with an abnormal ambition and an obsessive desire to stand out from the crowd and become an exceptional personality. He believed one of the means to achieve this goal was to make public appearances on television.

In the course of its work, the commission found no presence on the large anti-submarine warfare ship *Storozhevoy* of a hostile anti-Soviet group or the so-called revolutionary committee, which was mentioned in the telegram to the commander-in-chief of the Navy. SABLIN acted alone with the support of a few people whom he had suborned only on the eve of the open action. The assertion that SABLIN planned to take the ship to Sweden was not substantiated in the course of the investigation.

SABLIN comes across as somebody who has hidden his fervent anti-Sovietism and hostile views for a long time. Using demagogic means and the authority of his high position, and exploiting the insufficient political maturity, passivity, and indecision of a part of the crew, he succeeded for a short time in gaining control of the ship.

The commanding officer of the ship, Captain Second Rank A. V. POTUL'NYY, failed to train his crew to act as a united combat team capable of carrying out its soldierly duty in any situation. The investigation also revealed a distinct passivity and confusion among the ship's officers, who failed to recognize the anti-Soviet thought in the announcements and intentions of the traitor in time decisively to put an end to his activities.

With regard to the unauthorized departure of the ship, the duty officers and leadership of the Riga Naval Base were derelict in their duties. Having received a report from Senior Lieutenant V. V. FIRSOV, the chief of staff for the 78th Ship Security Brigade for the protection of the water area Captain Second Rank V. S. VLASOV; the head of the Brigade Special Detachment Captain Second Rank V. G. YUDIN; and roadstead duty officer and commanding officer of the submarine S-263 Captain Second Rank L. V. SVETLOVSKIY instead of taking the necessary measures conferred together for an extended period, greatly delayed in reporting to the command post, and displayed a lack of ability and indecisiveness bordering on cowardice.

We also report:

During the interviews of the commission and leading officers with many crew members, and also with all crewmen of the large anti-submarine warfare ship *Storozhevoy*, everybody expressed outrage at SABLIN's treacherous activities and asked to assure the Minister of Defence, the Central Committee of the Communist Party of the Soviet Union, and personally Comrade L. I. BREZHNEV that the sailors, petty officers, warrant officers, and officers deeply regret their temporary lack of vigilance and are ready to carry out their military duties.

Regarding the extraordinary event, an investigation is underway to bring the guilty parties to justice. A party meeting was held at which those most guilty, among them SABLIN, were expelled from the Communist Party of the Soviet Union. The ship's crew was disbanded, and the ship received a new crew. The large anti-submarine warfare ship *Storozhevoy* is available for duty, with weapons and technical equipment in good order. The Navy has taken measures to prevent information leakage.[6]

The report was signed by Admiral Gorshkov, as the chairman of the commission, and by the commission members: Aleksey Alekseyevich Yepishev, General of the Army; Pyotr Nikolayevich Navoytsev, Vice Admiral; Sergey Fyodorovich Romanov, Lieutenant General; Vladimir Dmitriyevich Sabaneyev, Rear Admiral; Yuriy Lyubanskiy, Major General; and Mikhail Ivanovich Gulyayev, Rear Admiral.

Gorshkov's commission report was blunt, almost crude, in its depiction of the anti-Soviet malice of Sablin, a lone wolf in sheep's clothing, as the sole reason for the incident. Nonetheless, the report concluded the investigation into the mutiny on the *Storozhevoy* as far as the Armed Forces were concerned. However, Sablin had been a political officer, and the ramifications of the mutiny for the Party were far more ominous than for the military. The Committee for State Security (KGB) had to find out exactly what had inspired Sablin, and yet more importantly, if he had more accomplices and followers than those already identified onboard the *Storozhevoy*.

On 18 February 1976, the KGB issued its report on the mutiny. Stamped Top Secret (*sovershenno sekretno*), it was directed to the Central Committee of the Communist Party of the Soviet Union. The report stated:

> The Committee for State Security concludes the investigation of a criminal case on the charge of Captain Third Rank V. M. SABLIN and other servicemen – participants in the criminal act that took place on 8-9 November 1975 on the large anti-submarine warfare ship *Storozhevoy* (14 people in total). It is established that SABLIN, the organizer of this crime, having fallen under the influence of revisionist ideology, over a number of years cultivated hostile views on Soviet reality. In April 1975, having formulated these views in writing, he recorded them on tape, and during the incident on the *Storozhevoy* gave an anti-Soviet speech to the personnel onboard. SABLIN's 'political platform' included a choice of slanderous assertions derived from bourgeois propaganda about the 'obsolescence' of Marxism-Leninism and the 'bureaucratic degeneration' of the state and party structures of the Soviet Union, appeals for the removal of the Communist Party of the Soviet Union from the leadership of our society, and the creation of a new, 'more progressive' party. In the spring of 1975, he developed a detailed plan to take over a warship, which he intended to use as a 'political podium' for putting forward demands for a change in the government structure of the Soviet Union and to fight against Soviet power.
>
> Preparing for the implementation of this plan, SABLIN studied the mood of the crew members, attached to himself individual servicemen, prepared them in the spirit of a negative attitude towards Soviet reality, however, as established by the investigation, he failed to find like-minded people and create an anti-Soviet group on the ship. Only three days before the events, SABLIN initiated the sailor A. N. SHEIN into his criminal plans, enlisted his support and handed over for distribution a magnetic tape with an anti-Soviet speech.
>
> Before being drafted into military service, SHEIN was prosecuted for participation in embezzlement, during his service he had 13 disciplinary sanctions, and made politically unhealthy judgments.
>
> During the events on the *Storozhevoy*, SHEIN, having received a pistol from SABLIN, assisted him in the arrest of the ship's commanding officer, took part in the isolation and putting under guard of officers and warrant officers who refused to support SABLIN, counteracted the attempts of individual crew members

to release the commanding officer and arrest SABLIN, at the same time inflicting bodily harm on petty officer KOPYLOV.

In order to involve part of the crew in illegal actions to gain control over the *Storozhevoy*, SABLIN used his official position as deputy commander for political affairs, and to disguise hostile intentions he resorted to sophisticated demagogic statements, accompanying them with quotes from the works of the classics of Marxism-Leninism.

As a result of SABLIN's criminal actions, the *Storozhevoy* was without authorisation moved from the Gulf of Riga beyond Soviet territorial waters towards Sweden (to within 21 nautical miles). SABLIN ignored the repeated and categorical demands of the command post to return the ship to the port. Only by decisive measures by the command post was the *Storozhevoy*, with the participation of members of her crew, stopped and returned to base. Thus, the large anti-submarine ship was removed from the contingent of the Navy available for combat for 16 hours.

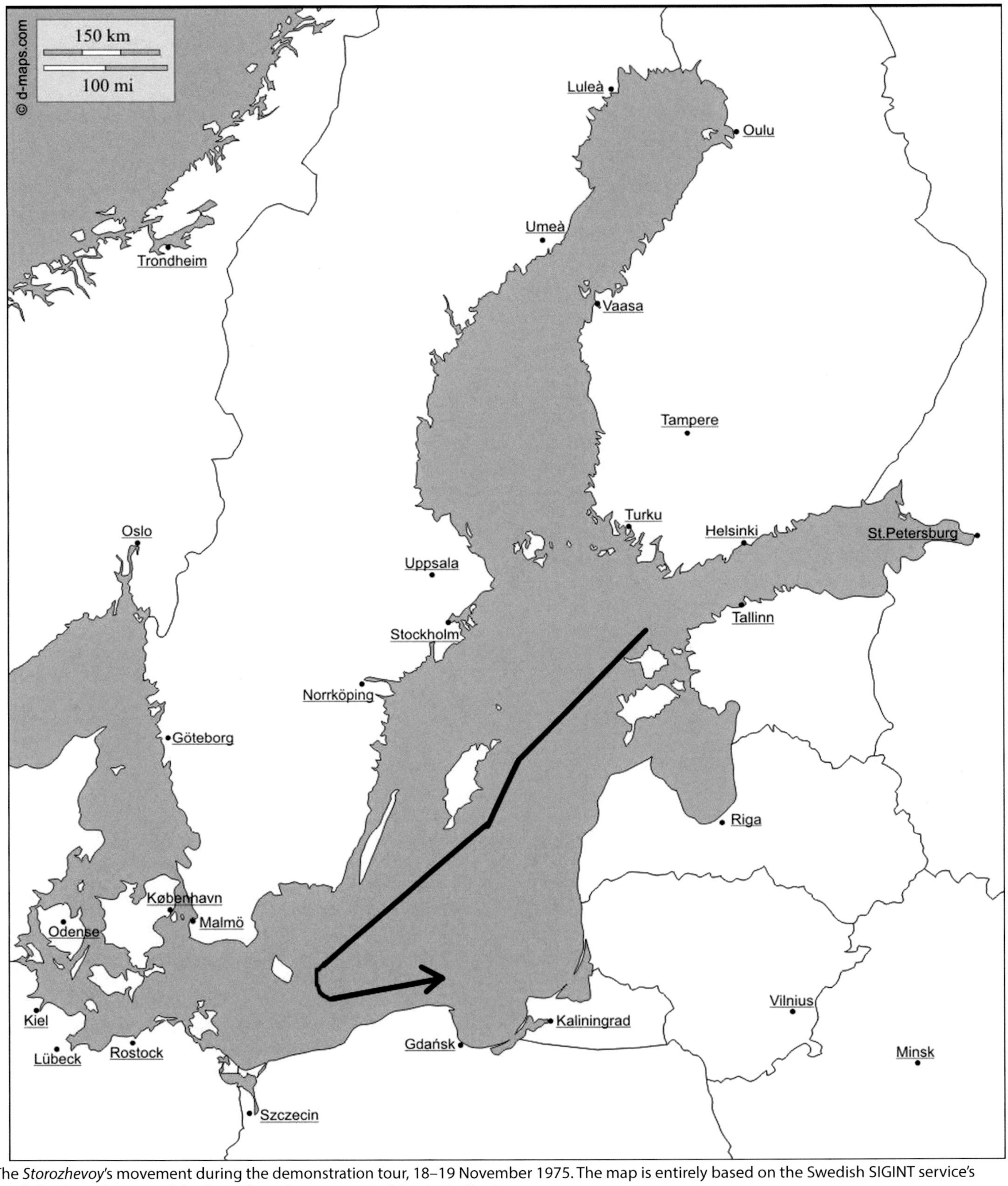

The *Storozhevoy*'s movement during the demonstration tour, 18–19 November 1975. The map is entirely based on the Swedish SIGINT service's carefully plotted course of the *Storozhevoy*'s movements. (Map by Author)

On the basis of the evidence obtained during the investigation, SABLIN's criminal activities qualify as treasonous, committed deliberately in order to undermine the existing system in the USSR and to the detriment of the military power of our country, while SHEIN's crime qualifies as aiding treason of the Motherland.

The rest of the accused: Lieutenants V. I. VAVILKIN and V. K. DUDNIK; warrant officers V. M. BORODAY, V. G. VELICHKO, A. A. GOMENCHUK, V. A. KALINICHEV, and A. T. KHOMYAKOV; Petty Officer A. V. SKIDANOV; Sailors V. N. AVERIN, M. M. BUROV, N. F. SALIVONCHIK, and G. V. SAKHNEVICH – young people aged 20–23, who still do not have sufficient life experience and political seasoning, were provoked and misled by SABLIN. They did not know about his treasonous plans, however, by supporting SABLIN's activities, they essentially helped him in the implementation of the criminal plan to seize the ship. Some of them at the initial stage refused to support SABLIN and were put in isolation by him. From the materials of the investigation, it can be seen that they had no intention to betray the Motherland, but due to the unexpectedness and short time of events, they did not understand in time the hostile direction of SABLIN's intentions and could not correctly assess them.

During interrogations, the indicated accused gave exhaustive testimony about the offenses committed, deeply regret their deeds, and condemn SABLIN's criminal adventure. Previously, they were not prosecuted for any criminal act.

The actions of this group of accused qualify as military crimes.

Taking into account the established circumstances and causes of the extraordinary events on the large anti-submarine warfare ship *Storozhevoy*, we consider it expedient to send the criminal case against SABLIN and SHEIN on charges of treason to the Motherland for consideration by the Military Collegium of the Supreme Court of the Soviet Union.

The remaining 12 accused – having committed military crimes in accordance with the ruling of the Presidium of the Supreme Soviet of the Soviet Union of 28 March 1958, the Decree of the Presidium of the Supreme Soviet of the Soviet Union of 28 March 1958, and the Decree of the Presidium of the Supreme Soviet of the Soviet Union of 26 November 1973, which regulate criminal proceedings against members of the Armed Forces – do not fall under the court's jurisdiction, their criminal cases are closed, and they are referred to disciplinary measures by the authority of the Minister of Defence of the Soviet Union.[7]

The KGB report was signed by the Chairman of the KGB, Yuriy Andropov; the Defence Minister, Andrey Grechko; the Procurator-General of the Soviet Union, Roman Andreyevich Rudenko; and the Chairman of the Supreme Court of the Soviet Union, Lev Nikolayevich Smirnov.

The KGB investigators clearly had to be cautious in how they phrased the report. It would not do to suggest that Sablin, in effect, had been more of a communist than the Communist Party leaders in his political programme. Instead, they fell back to the conclusion that Sablin's views derived from bourgeois propaganda, which was a more palatable view to the Party leadership. The KGB report also unequivocally placed the blame for the mutiny on Sablin and, to a significantly lesser degree, on Shein, who only grudgingly repented during the investigation. By this means, all the other arrested ringleaders could be handed over to the military authorities, which only would take disciplinary, not criminal, action against them.

The Baltic Fleet had not stood idle during the preparation of these reports. Something had to be done with the *Storozhevoy*, which clearly was the most obvious remaining piece of evidence of the mutiny which had taken place and the crisis that it had led to. The warship had suffered no major damage. The *Storozhevoy* remained in the southern part of the Gulf of Riga until 17 November 1975, that is, the same day when Admiral Gorshkov's commission issued its report to the Minister of Defence. Meanwhile, the warship was refurbished and any minor damage was repaired.

The Soviet leadership did its best to sweep the mutiny under the rug. Those involved were encouraged or threatened not to discuss the incident. A story was disseminated that the activity on 9 November had, in fact, been an exercise during which a specially prepared target barge had been attacked. The barge then drifted away, until Soviet units rediscovered it on

Sablin (left) and Potul'nyy. (Author's Collection)

11 November off Gotland, where it was again recovered by Soviet ships. However, the small disinformation campaign proved to be completely unnecessary, as no intelligence source at the time had drawn attention to the mutiny. No connection to the incident was therefore made until much later, and by then it was already clear that a mutiny really had taken place.[8]

Subsequently, during the period 18–19 November, the *Storozhevoy* carried out what was assessed by Swedish intelligence as a demonstration tour through the northern, central, and southern Baltic Sea. By all accounts, the warship passed through the difficult-to-navigate Moon Sound and then passed near Gotland, the Swedish naval base at Karlskrona, the Danish island of Bornholm, and the Polish coast. The FRA suspected, quite correctly, that the *Storozhevoy* then had a new crew. The purpose of the tour was probably to demonstrate that any Swedish, Danish, or Polish suspicions of mutiny would be unfounded, the Swedish Defence Staff noted.[9]

According to the original plan, the *Storozhevoy* was the following year transferred to the Pacific Fleet, where she remained until she was decommissioned in 2002. The *Storozhevoy* was then sold and scrapped in India in 2004.[10] In comparison, the older *Komsomolets Litvy*, whose damages were easily repaired, remained in service until 1987, when she was finally decommissioned.

Although none of the officers or warrant officers of the *Storozhevoy*, except Sablin, were prosecuted under criminal law, several were reduced in rank and some were dishonourably discharged, after formal demotion to the rank of ordinary sailor. Wartime regulations were applied, and some of those who were dishonourably discharged, including Senior Lieutenant Saitov and others who opposed the mutiny in various ways yet failed to use deadly force against the mutineers, in hindsight do not seem to have deserved such a punishment. The ship's commanding officer, Captain Second Rank Potul'nyy, was reduced in rank to Captain Third Rank and sent to serve in Tallinn Naval Base. After a year or two, he was restored to his previous rank. Potul'nyy ultimately retired as a Captain First Rank. However, he never again commanded a warship at sea. As for the officers named in Admiral Gorshkov's commission report, the only one who reportedly suffered no career setback in the Navy was Senior Lieutenant Firsov, who successfully escaped the *Storozhevoy* to report the mutiny.[11]

10
LESSONS LEARNED FOR SWEDISH INTELLIGENCE

Since the 1950s, the vast bulk of Swedish intelligence on Soviet air and naval units derived from SIGINT. In the case of the mutiny on the *Storozhevoy*, there was also HUMINT reporting, from an agent in place in Riga who contributed additional fragments of the event. In comparison, US intelligence, and for that matter other Western intelligence services, lacked access to relevant sources relating to the mutiny. However, intelligence sharing between Sweden and other Western partners took place on a regular basis, so eventually those Western countries which needed to know about the incident also learned of it. At first, the Western intelligence services chose not to publicise the event. However, when Milits, the handler of the agent in Riga, published the story in a newspaper, it was no longer possible to ignore the mutiny. Yet, while the news media reporting brought public attention to the incident, the political implications were minimal. In the Soviet Union, the mutiny remained buried in the KGB archives for almost 15 years.

Because the intelligence reports were only issued long after the event, the SIGINT reporting, despite its level of detail and considerable interest to a later historian, led to exactly nothing with regard to Swedish foreign policy. A major reason for this was that since the *Storozhevoy* ultimately surrendered, it never reached Swedish waters. Another reason was, perhaps, that the incident revealed weaknesses in Sweden's military preparedness and combat readiness. Since the mutiny took place on a weekend, neither the FRA nor the Swedish armed forces understood the nature and seriousness of the incident until after several days. For sure, FRA SIGINT collection operated around the clock, but in 1975, analysts worked regular office hours. SIGINT had been collected, voice communications had been recorded, but no real analysis took place until later. The situation was the same within other components of the Swedish intelligence community. Primarily based on SIGINT but with important contributions from HUMINT, Swedish intelligence had monitored the mutiny in great detail. Yet, since the mutiny took place during a weekend the Swedish Defence Staff had reacted slowly. Northern Europe had by then been at peace for decades, so complacence had permeated Swedish intelligence.

The mutiny on the *Storozhevoy* came as a surprise to everyone involved, from the commanding officer of the *Storozhevoy*, Potul'nyy, and the roadstead duty officer and commanding officer of the submarine S-263 next door, Svetlovskiy, all the way to the analysts at the FRA and the Swedish Navy Staff. At first no one could imagine that something so unexpected could happen. Therefore, it took time for someone to react, even though information about the mutiny actually became available in real time. This applied to the Soviet Baltic Fleet, and the same phenomenon could be observed within the Swedish intelligence community.

Wilhelm Agrell later noted that:

> Krivak 500 [the *Storozhevoy*] was for me associated with two surprises, which I pondered a lot afterwards. One was that I knew about the incident but did not react to it. I had not understood the meaning of the report on the bombing because the actual context went beyond what seemed reasonable to expect. The second surprise was then already known: no one had reacted when the incident took place. If the mutineers had succeeded in reaching Swedish waters, our decision-makers and the few military units on combat alert duty would not have had any advance warning which would have allowed them time to prepare a response adapted to the specific situation that arose.[1]

The FRA had, after all, noted the hunt for the mutineers and also recorded, and finally reported, most of the available radio traffic, yet the SIGINT agency had failed to give any kind of early warning. The fact that the military intelligence service had also missed the incident was not a consolation in this context. Nor that the intelligence services of the United States and the other NATO countries had failed to pay attention to it.

So, something needed to be done. Although presently detente characterised the relations between the Western and Eastern blocs, the Cold War was not far off. The FRA was expected to be able to fulfil the task of acting as an alarm bell, that is, to warn of attack preparations or an immediate threat of attack on Sweden. In the present case, although Sweden had not been directly threatened, it was hardly reassuring to note that the Soviet Union did not hesitate to carry out armed attacks just outside Gotland, even though the attacks were aimed against its own ships.

What had failed at the FRA was to quickly convey the intelligence picture to first its own headquarters on Lovön Island outside Stockholm, and then the Defence Staff. Those who had the greatest opportunity to report in real time were the collection officers at FRA's remote stations. They were the ones who noticed and, when possible, also recorded Soviet military radio traffic. It was reasonable to conclude that the collection officers should be given improved opportunities to report important events directly to the FRA headquarters on Lovön Island.

For this reason, after the *Storozhevoy* incident, the FRA on its own initiative began to introduce new and faster reporting procedures. The SIGINT agency realised that 24/7 operations were still needed, just like the FRA had operated during the Second World War. Various means were implemented to achieve this, and to ensure that no similar situation would occur.

A first step was to send short, rapid reports, so-called 'harpoons', directly from the intercept stations to the central processing and analysis unit on Lovön Island. It also became more common in the long run that the analysts at headquarters directed counter-questions to the intercept stations, which thus came to play an increasingly active role in the intelligence reporting. These measures were simple and did not require a major reorganisation or any time-consuming inventory of the agency's total resources before implementation. Nonetheless, they created a foundation for the FRA and thereby the Swedish intelligence community as a whole to significantly increase its capacity for intelligence collection and analysis. Thus, these simple matters significantly helped the Swedish intelligence community to enhance its capacity and ultimately reach its top performance during the latter half of the 1980s, with regard to intelligence on Soviet military activities in the geographical neighbourhood.[2] The mutiny on the *Storozhevoy* thus became the catalyst that the FRA needed to wake up after 30 years of peacetime operations which had created a situation of stagnation and disproportionate introspection, with the consequent excessive self-confidence and inability to act in the face of the unknown which often makes established intelligence organisations underperform when it really matters. Heeding the lessons of the *Storozhevoy* incident, Swedish intelligence streamlined operations which came to serve well for the rest of the Cold War.

With regard to the Swedish participants in the intelligence reporting on the *Storozhevoy* incident, Wilhelm Agrell eventually chose an academic career at Lund University, where he in time became Sweden's first professor of intelligence analysis. Jan Leijonhielm also came to follow the academic path, ultimately becoming head of Russian Studies at the Swedish Defence Research Agency (FOI) and member of the Royal Swedish Academy of War Sciences. Ulf Hugo worked with air force intelligence first at the Air Force Staff, and then the Defence Staff. In 1982, he moved on to the Defence Matériel Administration (FMV), where he continued to handle technical intelligence within the aerospace field until 2010, when he retired. Hugo has since described technical intelligence in two books. Alex Milits remained active in intelligence collection until he retired. He passed away in 2012. As for the SIGINT officer Rune Axelsson, he continued to monitor Soviet naval developments until he retired from the service in 1988. Sadly, he passed away soon after retirement.

As a final note, we should perhaps consider the civilian cargo ship *Volgo-Balt 38*, whose crew were the only civilians who came under fire during the mutiny on the *Storozhevoy*. Built in 1968 in Gorkiy (since 1990 again known as Nizhniy Novgorod), she survived the air strike in 1975 but fate caught up with her in 1993, off the Bulgarian port of Varna in the Black Sea. She ran aground, broke in two, and sank.

NOTES ON SOURCES

The first book-length account of the mutiny on the *Storozhevoy* was written in 1982 by Gregory D. Young, when he as a lieutenant in the U.S. Navy completed a master's degree on the mutiny, published as *Mutiny on Storozhevoy: A Case Study of Dissent in the Soviet Navy* (Monterey: Naval Postgraduate School, 1982). Young's dissertation later inspired the fiction writer Thomas L. Clancy, Jr. to write the novel *The Hunt for Red October* (1984).[1]

It was only in 1990 that the Soviet Union publicly acknowledged that the mutiny on the *Storozhevoy* even had taken place. By then it was too late to determine the exact course of events based on Soviet archive documents. Most had been destroyed, and key participants in the event had passed away.

This did not prevent the publication of a number of books and television documentaries in English and Russian on the mutiny. Among them, two should be singled out as particularly notable. Gregory D. Young's and Nate Braden's *The Last Sentry: The True Story that Inspired The Hunt for Red October* (Annapolis: Naval Institute Press, 2005) gives an excellent description of the events surrounding the mutiny, although the additional perspective offered by real-time SIGINT intercepts is missing. Young and Braden worked with the late Sablin's family, which means that their work is particularly good on his personal situation and circumstances. In Russian, the best work is Vladimir V. Shigin's *Myatezhnyy 'Storozhevoy': Posledniy parad kapitana 3-ego ranga Sablina* (Moscow: Veche, 2013), which has the additional advantage of being based on research carried out in the Russian security service FSB's archive. Since the FSB is the successor of the Soviet KGB, the FSB archive safeguards logbooks and other documents from the Border Troops. For obvious reasons, Shigin's book, too, lacks the added perspective of real-time SIGINT intercepts. Of these two books, the one by Young and Braden paints a quite sympathetic picture of Sablin. In contrast, Shigin's book gives a somewhat less compassionate take on Sablin's character and aims.

Nikolay Cherkashin's early Russian-language book *Posledniy parad: Khronika antibrezhnevskogo myatezha* (Moscow: Andreyevskiy flag, 1992) should be mentioned as well. Cherkashin was another former political officer in the Soviet Navy, knew Sablin's family, and regarded Sablin as a hero. Beginning in 1989, Cherkashin attempted to use Mikhail Gorbachev's new glasnost policy to publish his take on the mutiny in a number of Soviet newspapers. Even so, it took him some effort to get the story published.[2] Cherkashin has since published many of the documents relating to the *Storozhevoy* mutiny online, at the web site https://unotices.com/books-u/92567.

Among the television documentaries produced to depict the events surrounding the mutiny, an early one was *Russkaya tragediya* (Moscow: Ekran veka, 1993). Interesting interviews with some of the participants can also be found in *Mutiny: The True Story of Red October* (Channel Four, 2000); *Posledniy parad zampolita Sablina* (VIP Tekniks, 2008); and *The True Story: The Hunt for Red October* (History Channel, n.d.). Several documentaries are available online.

However, because of the destruction of documents relating to the air units involved in the *Storozhevoy* incident, neither of the existing works is able to provide a full description of the events during the mutiny. For this, we have to go to the FRA archive, which holds the SIGINT reporting on the *Storozhevoy* mutiny. As we have seen, the SIGINT reporting enables an in-detail understanding of the event and provides a means to assess the real facts and significance of it. There is no previous book in either English or Russian which takes advantage of the FRA real-time SIGINT intercepts. Until now, the events described in these sources were only published in two Swedish-language works by the present author: Michael Fredholm von Essen's *Myteriet på Storozjevoj 1975: FRA och Krivakincidenten* (Bromma: FRA, Historiska skrifter 21, 2014) and *Hemligstämplat: Svensk underrättelsetjänst från Erlander till Bildt* (Stockholm: Medström, 2020).

For the historian, the FRA reporting brings significant benefits. Despite the previous books and television documentaries, there was hitherto no means to verify what the eyewitnesses claimed to have taken place. First, the Soviet authorities because of the very nature of the mutiny had no means to clarify everything that happened before the mutiny was suppressed. Even in the court martial of Sablin and Shein, the Soviet authorities often had to take their words for what had happened. For the time period before the warship was located by KGB Border Troops and Naval Aviation, the Soviet authorities could not even determine its exact route. They were literally out of the loop of what was taking place aboard the *Storozhevoy* or even, before the ship was located, where it was and where it was headed.

Furthermore, we have seen that the participants according to several eyewitnesses were ordered to destroy any documentation of the incident as seen from a Frontal Aviation or Naval Aviation perspective.

As a result, the FRA reporting on the incident provides the only comprehensive view of the entire incident. Without it, modern-day researchers, whether in Russia or elsewhere, would know far less of the event.

NOTES

Chapter 1

1 Sergey A. Gulyayev, 'Rol' aviatsii v boyevykh operatsiyakh na more v sovremennykh usloviyakh', *Morskoy sbornik* 6, 1965, pp.36–43.

2 Robert B. Bathurst, *Understanding the Soviet Navy: A Hand Book* (Newport, Rhode Island: Naval War College Press, 1979), p.127.

3 V. G. Yefremenko, 'Razvitiye i sovershenstvovaniye protivolodochnykh sil i ikh taktiki', *Morskoy sbornik* 10, 1970, pp.16–23.

4 Sergey G. Gorshkov, *Morskaya moshch' gosudarstva* (Moscow: Voyenizdat, 1976), p.359. Gorshkov's book is known in the West as 'The Military Might of the State'.

5 Bathurst, *Understanding the Soviet Navy*, pp.xiv-xv.

6 Ibid., p.39.

7 Gorshkov, *Morskaya moshch' gosudarstva*, p.315.

8 See, e.g., John Jordan, *An Illustrated Guide to the Modern Soviet Navy* (London: Salamander Books, 1982), p.8, which otherwise gives a for its time authoritative description of the Soviet Navy.

9 Michael Fredholm von Essen, 'When Intelligence Made a Difference: How Sweden Chose Sides', *Intelligencer Journal* (AFIO, 2019), pp.41–43. For full details (in Swedish), see Michael Fredholm von Essen, *Hemligstämplat: Svensk underrättelsetjänst från Erlander till Bildt* (Stockholm: Medström, 2020).

10 Bathurst, *Understanding the Soviet Navy*, pp.xv-xvi.

11 Unlike in the West, Soviet practice was always to refer to warships in masculine, not feminine, form.

12 Vladimir V. Shigin, *Myatezhnyy 'Storozhevoy': Posledniy parad kapitana 3-ego ranga Sablina* (Moscow: Veche, 2013), p.58.

13 From various, sometimes conflicting, sources.

14 Shigin, *Myatezhnyy 'Storozhevoy'*, pp.333–334.

15 Former *Storozhevoy* warrant officer Viktor Boroday; cited in Shigin, *Myatezhnyy 'Storozhevoy'*, p.155.

16 Vladimir G. Yegorov, *Vakhtu sdal ispravno* (Kaliningrad: IP Mishutkina I. V., 2008), Vol. 1, p.24. Yegorov served in the 128th Missile Ship Brigade at the time of the mutiny. From 1991 to 2000, he was the last commanding officer of the Soviet Baltic Fleet and the first commanding officer of the Russian Federation's Baltic Fleet. From 2000 to 2005, Yegorov served as Governor of Kaliningrad.

17 Captain first rank was in the Soviet Navy the equivalent rank of a Royal Navy commodore or a U.S. Navy rear admiral, lower half.

18 Notably *Krasnaya zvezda*, 24 December 1974.

19 Gregory D. Young and Nate Braden, *The Last Sentry: The True Story that Inspired The Hunt for Red October* (Annapolis: Naval Institute Press, 2005), pp.56–58, 193–196, which also provides a translation of the article into English.

Chapter 2

1 Captain third rank was in the Soviet Navy the equivalent rank of a Royal Navy or U.S. Navy commander or an army or air force lieutenant colonel.

2 Shigin, *Myatezhnyy 'Storozhevoy'*, p.338.

3 Young and Braden, *Last Sentry*, p.21; Shigin, *Myatezhnyy 'Storozhevoy'*, pp.26–27.

4 According to the subsequent testimony of Sablin, 22 March 1976; cited by Shigin, *Myatezhnyy 'Storozhevoy'*, p.141.

5 Young and Braden, *Last Sentry*, pp.81, 83–86; which also gives a good overall description of conscript life in the Soviet Navy.

6 Yegorov, *Vakhtu sdal ispravno*, p.28.

7 Young and Braden, *Last Sentry*, p.vii.

8 Young and Braden, *Last Sentry*, pp.124, 135; Shigin, *Myatezhnyy 'Storozhevoy'*, pp.148–149.

9 That is, the package with the tape recording remained in her possession until, after the eventual arrest and interrogation of Shein a few days later, the KGB paid her a visit to retrieve it. The girl never opened the package. Shigin, *Myatezhnyy 'Storozhevoy'*, pp.174–175.

10 Even the KGB could not find out anything beyond what Sablin eventually admitted to during interrogation. Shigin, *Myatezhnyy 'Storozhevoy'*, p.176.

11 All reported times are Moscow time, which was standard time in the Soviet Baltic Fleet.

12 Shigin, *Myatezhnyy 'Storozhevoy'*, pp.177, 186.

13 Captain second rank was in the Soviet Navy the equivalent rank of a Royal Navy or U.S. Navy captain.

14 Young and Braden, *Last Sentry*, pp.5, 98; Shigin, *Myatezhnyy 'Storozhevoy'*, p.227.

Chapter 3

1 Interview with one of the mutineers, in *Mutiny: The True Story of Red October* (Channel Four, 2000).

2 Shigin, *Myatezhnyy 'Storozhevoy'*, pp.230–232.

3 Yegorov, *Vakhtu sdal ispravno*, p.29. From this point, the description of the course of events during the mutiny is, unless otherwise mentioned, based on SIGINT reporting from the FRA archive. Michael Fredholm von Essen, *Myteriet på Storozjevoj 1975: FRA och Krivakincidenten* (Bromma: FRA, Historiska skrifter 21, 2014).

4 Shigin, *Myatezhnyy 'Storozhevoy'*, p.236.

5 Shigin, *Myatezhnyy 'Storozhevoy'*, p.236.

6 Various, sometimes conflicting sources.

7 Shigin, *Myatezhnyy 'Storozhevoy'*, p.66.

8 Shigin, *Myatezhnyy 'Storozhevoy'*, pp.263–264.

9 Various, sometimes conflicting sources.

10 Shigin, *Myatezhnyy 'Storozhevoy'*, pp.260, 265, 266, 268.

11 After the event, there were claims that Neypert refused to open fire on the mutineers, because he did not regard them as enemies. Young and Braden, *Last Sentry*, p.108; various web sites, including the 44th Missile Regiment's *Bunt na BPK Storozhevoy* (http://rocketpolk44.narod.ru). There were also claims that Neypert for this reason lost his command and was transferred to the reserve. However, Neypert was an old officer, and his transfer to the reserve may well have been the effect of his age and for this reason no extraordinary event. Shigin, *Myatezhnyy 'Storozhevoy'*, p.397.

12 Various, sometimes conflicting sources.

13 The telegram is reprinted in Shigin, *Myatezhnyy 'Storozhevoy'*, pp.246–247, 406–407.

14 Shigin, *Myatezhnyy 'Storozhevoy'*, pp.319–320.

15 According to the subsequent testimony of Sablin, 13 January 1976; cited in Shigin, *Myatezhnyy 'Storozhevoy'*, pp.317–318.

16 The telegram is reprinted in Shigin, *Myatezhnyy 'Storozhevoy'*, pp.251–252.

17 Shigin, *Myatezhnyy 'Storozhevoy'*, p.268.

18 Young and Braden, *Last Sentry*, p.100; citing an interview in the documentary *Russkaya tragediya* (Moscow: Ekran veka, 1993).

19 Yegorov, *Vakhtu sdal ispravno*, p.29.

20 Jan-Olof Grahn, *FRA och det kalla krigets början: Signalunderrättelsetjänsten 1945-1960* (Bromma: FRA, Historiska skrifter 20, 2013), pp.25–26.
21 Pleškys commanded a submarine tender. For information on other mutinies in the Soviet Navy, see Young and Braden, *Last Sentry*, pp.165–167.

Chapter 4

1 Personal communication from a former Soviet Naval Aviation officer.
2 Various, sources.
3 The Central Intelligence Agency (CIA) acquired a copy of the classified series of doctrinal documents, which the Agency then translated and analyzed. Parts of the translation have been declassified. CIA, *Soviet Naval Strategy and Its Effect on the Development of Naval Forces 1953-1963*, report dated 22 October 1963. It takes time to change an existing military doctrine and introduce new weapon systems, so in 1975 the Soviet Armed Forces remained dimensioned after the threat as it was perceived during the 1960s.
4 CIA, *Soviet Naval Strategy*, pp.66, 68–69.
5 CIA, *Soviet Naval Strategy*, pp.70–71, 78, 80.
6 Technical specifications have been declassified. See, e.g., the web site *Aviatsionnaya entsiklopediya ugolok neba*, www.airwiki.org.
7 Carlo Kopp, *Maritime Strike: The Soviet Perspective* (Air Power Australia, 2005); Carlo Kopp, "Soviet Cruise Missiles Post World War II", *Defence Today*, December 2008, pp.43–45; the web site *Aviatsionnaya entsiklopediya ugolok neba*, www.airwiki.org.
8 Aleksandr Georgiyevich Tsymbalov, 'Vooruzhonnyy myatezh na Baltflote', *Nezavisimoye voyennoye obozreniye*, 20 August 2004. The future Major General Tsymbalov served as deputy chief of staff of the 668th Bomber Aviation Regiment during the crisis and participated in the mission.
9 Shigin, *Myatezhnyy 'Storozhevoy'*, pp.279, 326.

Chapter 5

1 Tsymbalov, 'Vooruzhonnyy myatezh na Baltflote'.
2 Young and Braden, *Last Sentry*, p.103
3 Various, sometimes conflicting sources.
4 Tsymbalov, 'Vooruzhonnyy myatezh na Baltflote'.
5 Young and Braden, *Last Sentry*, p.105; citing Nikolay Cherkashin, *Posledniy parad: Khronika antibrezhnevskogo myatezha* (Moscow: Andreyevskiy flag, 1992).
6 Tsymbalov, 'Vooruzhonnyy myatezh na Baltflote'.
7 *Aviatsiya i vremya* 2, 1998; information from Major General Valeriy Yevdokimovich Ognev, who served in the regiment. Web site, www.forumavia.ru, November 2007.
8 Shigin, *Myatezhnyy 'Storozhevoy'*, p.288.
9 Tsymbalov, 'Vooruzhonnyy myatezh na Baltflote'.
10 As noted, Soviet practice was always to refer to warships in masculine, not feminine, form.
11 Shigin, *Myatezhnyy 'Storozhevoy'*, p.289.
12 Tsymbalov, 'Vooruzhonnyy myatezh na Baltflote'.

Chapter 6

1 Interview with Colonel General Gulyayev, in *Mutiny: The True Story of Red October* (Channel Four, 2000). The interview is also cited in Young and Braden, *Last Sentry*, p.102. Incidentally, both the television documentary and the book misinterpret Gulyayev, who describes his communication with the Tu-16K commander Savinkov, not the Yak-28 commander Porotikov. Even though Gulyayev does not say it in plain words, the context indicates that he in the interview refers to the incident, described below, with Savinkov's alleged radar malfunction.
2 Shigin, *Myatezhnyy 'Storozhevoy'*, pp.273, 287.
3 Personal communication from a former Soviet Naval Aviation officer.
4 The eyewitness was the future Vice Admiral A. I. Korniyenko; cited in Shigin, *Myatezhnyy 'Storozhevoy'*, p.301.

Chapter 7

1 Yegorov, *Vakhtu sdal ispravno*, p.29; Shigin, *Myatezhnyy 'Storozhevoy'*, p.396.
2 Shigin, *Myatezhnyy 'Storozhevoy'*, pp.297–301.
3 Shigin, *Myatezhnyy 'Storozhevoy'*, p.302–303.
4 Shigin, *Myatezhnyy 'Storozhevoy'*, p.260; Yegorov, *Vakhtu sdal ispravno*, p.27.
5 Shigin, *Myatezhnyy 'Storozhevoy'*, p.305.

Chapter 8

1 Michael Fredholm von Essen, 'Guide to the Study of Intelligence: Sweden's Intelligence Services', *Intelligencer Journal*, AFIO, 2015. For more details (in Swedish), see Michael Fredholm von Essen, *Underrättelsetjänstens villkor* (Bromma: FRA, 2016).
2 Michael Fredholm von Essen, *The Lion from the North – The Swedish Army during the Thirty Years War: Volume 1, 1618–1632* (Warwick: Helion, 2020), pp.224–233.
3 Tage Erlander, *Dagböcker 1945–1949* (Hedemora: Gidlunds, 2001), pp.160–161. The Prime Minister's diaries, subsequently published.
4 For further information in English, see Alexander Mull, *Notes on the Wennerström Case* (CIA Historical Review Program, 22 September 1993; web site www.cia.gov/library/center-for-the-study-of-intelligence/kent-csi/vol10no3/html/v10i3a07p_0001.htm); or Thomas Whiteside, *An Agent in Place: The Wennerström Affair* (New York: The Viking Press, 1966).
5 Personal communication from Gunno Gunnvall, a former FRA officer who subsequently served as head of radar intelligence, October 2013.
6 Wilhelm Agrell, *Konsten att gissa rätt: Underrättelsevetenskapens grunder* (Lund: Studentlitteratur, 1998), p.194; Wilhelm Agrell, 'Intelligence Analysis after the Cold War: New Paradigm or Old Anomalies?', Gregory F. Treverton and Wilhelm Agrell (eds), *National Intelligence Systems: Current Research and Future Prospects* (Cambridge: Cambridge University Press, 2009), pp.93–114.
7 Personal communication from Wilhelm Agrell, October 2013.
8 Agrell, *Konsten att gissa rätt*, p.194.
9 The Swedish radar intelligence service always recorded the plan position indicator (PPI) radar images on film. The films showing the Yak-28 flights have been declassified and made available on a DVD (known as *Ljuspunkter i mörkret: Ett urval av PPI-filmer*) from the web site of the organisation Försvarets Historiska Telesamlingar (www.fht.nu). The films can also be viewed on the web site, as well as on YouTube.
10 Personal communication from Jan Leijonhielm, October 2013. Birgitta Milits, the widow of the late Alex Milits, after her husband's death confirmed the events and agreed to the publication of her late husband's until then covert links to Swedish intelligence. The events were previously also briefly described in Agrell, 'Intelligence Analysis after the Cold War', p.107, n.21.
11 Personal communications from Alex Milits to Gregory Young, 7 December 1981 and 2 February 1982. Young and Braden, *Last Sentry*, pp.140–141. The initial misunderstanding of the name is confirmed by the intelligence reporting from Milits. Otherwise,

much of his information to Young was fiction invented to hide his real sources.

12 'Possible Mutiny Onboard Soviet Naval Ship', U.S. Defense Attaché's Office, Stockholm, 29 January 1976. The information about the report derives from Young and Braden, *Last Sentry,* pp.143, 144, 147–148.

13 Swedish National Archives (RA), Överbefälhavaren, Extra orientering (EXO) 7, 8 March 1976, Und H 810 (H 19). The report has since been declassified by the Foreign Ministry and reprinted in facsimile in Sven Fredrik Hedin, 'Myteriet i Riga', *Kungl Krigsvetenskapsakademiens handlingar och tidskrift* 1997: 6, pp.157–163.

14 Milits's source mentioned that a warship had been damaged. The FRA reporting lacked this information, but it noted that the aircraft had released bombs as close as 50 metres ahead of the *Komsomolets Litvy*.

15 Swedish National Archives (RA), Överbefälhavaren, Extra orientering (EXO) 7, 8 March 1976, Und H 810 (H 19). Declassified by the Foreign Ministry.

16 Years later, Milits claimed that an anonymous Soviet sailor had read his first article and four days later called to tell him the identity of the ship on which the mutiny had taken place. Personal communications from Alex Milits to Gregory Young, 7 December 1981 and 2 February 1982. Young and Braden, *Last Sentry,* p.141. In this manner, Milits hid his real sources. Milits still carried out clandestine work for Swedish intelligence at the time of his contacts with Young and had no intention to expose his sources of information.

17 *Svenska Dagbladet,* 5 May 1976, pp.1, 10.

18 *Svenska Dagbladet,* 14 May 1976, p.34.

19 Andrey A. Grechko, *The Armed Forces of the Soviet State: A Soviet View* (Washington, DC: United States Government Printing Office, 1978), p.86. Grechko's book was first published in Russian in 1975. The English translation is, unexpectedly, the final edition of Grechko's work, because it was based on revisions which Grechko made shortly before his death in 1976. The revised edition was apparently never published in Russian.

20 Tsymbalov, 'Vooruzhonnyy myatezh na Baltflote'.

21 Personal communication from a former Soviet Naval Aviation officer.

22 Personal communication from a Naval Aviation veteran.

23 Interview with Colonel General Gulyayev, in *Mutiny: The True Story of Red October* (Channel Four, 2000).

24 With thanks to Johan Claeson, who first suggested this interpretation, which is supported by tactical advice in CIA, *Soviet Naval Strategy*, p.80.

25 Personal communications from former Soviet airmen.

26 Personal communication from the family of a former Soviet Naval Aviation officer.

Chapter 9

1 According to the subsequent testimony of Sablin, 13 January 1976; cited in Shigin, *Myatezhnyy 'Storozhevoy'*, pp.317–318.

2 Young and Braden, *Last Sentry,* p.128.

3 Grechko, *Armed Forces of the Soviet State*, p.348.

4 Young and Braden, *Last Sentry,* pp.118, 127, 128, 130.

5 Interview with Colonel General Gulyayev, in *Mutiny: The True Story of Red October* (Channel Four, 2000).

6 The report is reprinted in Shigin, *Myatezhnyy 'Storozhevoy'*, pp.311–314.

7 The report, dated 18 February 1976 and apparently registered as legal act 408-A of the Central Committee of the Communist Party of the Soviet Union, is reprinted, in part, in Shigin, *Myatezhnyy 'Storozhevoy'*, pp.354–355. The entire report is available online, e.g., in Nikolay Cherkashin's web site, https://unotices.com/books-u/92567/. Although the report thus has been published several times, the original seems not to have been officially released. The various published versions for this reason differ in minor details.

8 Young and Braden, *Last Sentry,* pp.118, 133, 143, 209. Young received the information about the barge from Alex Milits.

9 Swedish National Archives (RA), Överbefälhavaren, Extra orientering (EXO) 7, 8 March 1976, Und H 810 (H 19). Declassified by the Foreign Ministry.

10 Yegorov, *Vakhtu sdal ispravno,* p.28.

11 Shigin, *Myatezhnyy 'Storozhevoy'*, pp.392–397.

Chapter 10

1 Agrell, *Konsten att gissa rätt*, p.195.

2 It was not only the FRA which reached its top performance during the latter half of the 1980s. The same applied to most of the Swedish intelligence community. See, e.g., Jerk Fehling, *Flygunderrättelseboken: Inblickar i flygteknik och underrättelsetjänst* (Stockholm, 2007), p.171.

Notes on Sources

1 On the background and link to Clancy's novel, see Young and Braden, *Last Sentry,* pp.149–150. Perhaps Clancy should have taken inspiration from the aforementioned Lithuanian defector Jonas Pleškys instead of the Marxist Valeriy Sablin.

2 For more details on how public awareness of the mutiny grew, see Young and Braden, *Last Sentry,* pp.151–155.

ABOUT THE AUTHOR

Professor Michael Fredholm von Essen is an historian and former military analyst who has published extensively on the history, defence strategies, security policies, intelligence services, issues related to terrorism, and energy sector developments of Eurasia. He lectured, during conferences or as visiting professor, at numerous institutions and universities around the world, and also led the team which developed the lone actor terrorism counter-strategy and training programme for the Swedish Police Authority. Michael Fredholm von Essen has published a large number of books, including *Afghanistan Beyond the Fog of War* (Copenhagen: NIAS Press, 2018); *Transnational Organized Crime and Jihadist Terrorism: Russian-Speaking Networks in Western Europe* (London: Routledge, 2016); and several books on military history for Helion & Company.